Perspectives on Conservative Criminal Justice Reform

DISCUSSIONS ABOUT REFORM IN 2015

Center for Effective Justice
TEXAS PUBLIC POLICY FOUNDATION
901 Congress Avenue | Fourth Floor
Austin, TX 78701

Including contributions from

GOV. SAM BROWNBACK | GROVER NORQUIST | JULIE STEWART
PAT NOLAN | SEN. JOHN WHITMIRE | SEN. JOSE RODRIGUEZ
BILL MONTGOMERY | ADAM GELB | MARC LEVIN
REP. JAMES WHITE | REP. TAN PARKER
TONY FABELO | CHELSEA BUCHHOLTZ | DEREK COHEN
LEON EVANS | COLLEEN HORTON | ANDREW KELLER | KATE MURPHY

introduction by DIANNA MULDROW

Perspectives on Conservative Criminal Justice Reform is published in the United States by Right on Crime, a project of the Texas Public Policy Foundation in partnership with the American Conservative Union Foundation and the Justice Fellowship.

TEXAS PUBLIC POLICY FOUNDATION
901 Congress Avenue| Austin, TX 78701
For more information, please see rightoncrime.com

Book prepared for publication by David Reaboi

Contents

Introduction **7**

Criminal Justice Reform: Getting More Safety for Our Tax Dollars **9**
    Pat Nolan 9
    Gov. Sam Brownback 13
    Grover Norquist 15
    Julie Stewart 17
    Marc Levin 20
    Q&A 23

Texas Prison Reform 2.0 .... **26**
    Marc Levin 27
    Adam Gelb 28
    Bill Montgomery 35
    Sen. John Whitmire 45
    Rep. Tan Parker 48
    Q&A 51

21st Century Juvenile Justice: A Texas-Sized Problem **60**
    Derek Cohen 60
    Dr. Tony Fabelo 63
    Chelsea Buchholtz 66
    Sen. Jose Rodriguez 69
    Rep. James White 73

Rethinking Mental Health:
Are We Throwing the Right Life Lines to People with Mental Illness? **77**
    Kate Murphy 77
    Leon Evans 80
    Colleen Horton 85
    Andrew Keller 90
    Q&A 95

About Right on Crime **98**
    Our Statement Of Principles 98
    The Conservative Case for Criminal Justice Reform 102

Introduction

Dianna Muldrow
Texas Public Policy Foundation

In the last decade the right has become the leaders in criminal justice reform. The issue affects many of the values of the conservative movement, such as public safety and limited government. State after state has emphasized public safety and limited government by promoting alternative measures for low-risk offenders and prioritizing precious prison space for violent and high-risk offenders. The results have been falling crime rates, incarceration rates, and savings in the hundreds of millions.

Right on Crime has performed a key function in this process. In 2010, the Texas Public Policy Foundation and Director Marc Levin founded Right on Crime to voice conservative thought on criminal justice issues. Originally focusing on issues specific to Texas, Right on Crime researched and recommended reforms, facilitating discussion – as they are doing in the pages following – while great policy shifts occurred in the state. Adult and juvenile facilities closed, alternative sentences were strengthened, and the state avoided projected taxpayer expenses that were in the billions. Jerry Madden, the Chair of the House Corrections Committee at the time, and one of the primary mover and shakers in Texas criminal justice has since become a Senior Fellow with Right on Crime, staying very involved as the organization expands to other states as well as the federal level.

At Policy Orientation, a biannual gathering in Austin with the Texas Public Policy Foundation, Right on Crime gathered Texas legislators and stakeholders to discuss upcoming issues in the state's criminal justice system. Juvenile justice, the intersection of mental health and criminal justice, as well as sentencing reform were among the topics lined up, allowing legislators to hear arguments for and against policies before the upcoming legislative session. Concerned citizens and representatives of interested organizations attended and participated in a Question and Answer session.

Right on Crime has expanded beyond the realm of Texas, however, providing research and recommendations in states across the country. From "Controlling Costs and Protecting Public Safety in the Cornhusker State" by Marc Levin in Nebraska to op-eds by Right on Crime signatories such as Newt Gingrich and Grover Norquist in Georgia and Wisconsin, the organization is branching into new territory. A new office in Oklahoma has been added that is intended to focus on that state in the upcoming years.

The group is also making strides in federal areas. Kansas Governor Sam Brownback, Director of Families Against Mandatory Minimums Julie Stewart, Grover Norquist, and Marc Levin all converged at CPAC to bring these issues to light with a conservative perspective. The discussion reprinted here highlights these areas that Right on Crime will soon begin discussing on a federal level. Issues such as regulatory Overcriminalization, and limited government are as much if not more applicable on a federal level.

Conservative criminal justice reform is sweeping the nation, and Right on Crime is giving it a substantial push. In the few years since its foundation, the organization has wrought change in Texas and beyond. From state to federal, this movement is bringing conservative leaders to the table and bringing their values to taxpayers.

Criminal Justice Reform: Getting More Safety for Our Tax Dollars
GOV. SAM BROWNBACK | GROVER NORQUIST | MARC LEVIN | JULIE STEWART
MODERATOR: **PAT NOLAN**

This event took place at CPAC 2015.

Pat Nolan

Director, Center for Criminal Justice Reform, American Conservative Union Foundation Outreach Director, Right on Crime

PAT NOLAN *is a leading voice on criminal justice reform, highlighting the skyrocketing costs of prison, fiscal responsibility in the criminal justice system and reforms for non-violent offenders. He served for 15 years in the California State Assembly, four of those as the Assembly Republican Leader. He was a leader on crime issues, particularly on behalf of victims' rights, was one of the original sponsors of the Victims' Bill of Rights (Proposition 15), and was awarded the "Victims Advocate Award" by Parents of Murdered Children. Nolan was targeted for prosecution for a campaign contribution he accepted which turned out to be part of an FBI sting. He pleaded guilty to one count of racketeering and served 29 months in federal custody. Nolan is the author of* When Prisoners Return, *which describes the important role of the Church in helping prisoners get back on their feet after they are released. He is a frequent expert witness at Congressional hearings on important issues such as prison work programs, juvenile justice, prison safety, offender reintegration and religious freedom. He has lectured at many judicial conferences and legal conventions. He has coauthored articles for the Notre Dame Law School Journal of Law, Ethics and Public Policy and the Regent Law School Law Review. Nolan was member of the National Prison Rape Elimination Commission, appointed by the Speaker of the House of Representatives. He also served on the National Commission on Safety and Abuse in America's Prisons. Nolan was honored by the Freda Utley Foundation, the first American to receive this prestigious international honor. He also received the Justice Roundtable's Advocate Award for his "tireless work championing criminal justice reform." His opinion pieces have appeared in numerous periodicals including the Washington Post, the Los Angeles Times, the National Law Journal, National Review Online, and the Washington Times. Pat earned both his Bachelor of Arts in Political Science and his Juris Doctorate at the University of Southern California. Pat and his wife Gail have three children. The Nolans live in Leesburg, Virginia and are members of the St. John the Apostle Parish.*

As we speak, there are two million American behind bars. That is one out of every one hundred adult Americans. Adding probation and parole, it is 1 out of every 31 Americans. That is an astounding amount of power for the government to exercise. Of course we need prisons; there are a lot of people that do terrible things. Unfortunately, we have expanded prisons to include offenses that are not morally reprehensible. Some of these offenses are bad simply because the legislature says they are. Prison is for people that we are afraid of, not the ones we are mad at. The system has a forty percent recidivism rate. The system fails, and forty percent of those involved are back within three years. That doesn't keep us safe. We spend eighty-five billion dollars and we are not getting the public safety that we pay for. Prisons are the only institution that expands by failing. The more they fail, the more they expand—and the more they cost us taxpayers. Prisons are the second fastest growing portion of state budgets, second only to Medicaid. They eat up money that could go to roads, schools, or tax rebates. It gobbles up so much money, all while doing a terrible job.

We are honored to have Governor Brownback of Kansas here today. He was a champion of criminal justice reform long before it was cool for conservatives to be for it. He has been the catalyst behind every major effort in criminal justice reform in Kansas in the last fifteen years, either when he was in the House, the Senate, as well as now that he is the Governor. Without his leadership, we would not have had the Prison Rape Elimination act, or the Second Chance Act. Now he is facing the challenge of reforming the Department of Corrections in Kansas. He is very capable, very policy oriented, and very smart politically.

Governor Brownback has shown practical solutions with conservative principles. Dr. King said, "To change someone, you must first love them, and they must know that they are being loved." These mentoring programs show that people love people; government programs do not. Matching these people helps them with difficult decisions, and keeps them on the straight and narrow.

To his right is Marc Levin, the Director of Policy for the Center for

Effective Justice at the Texas Public Policy Foundation. Marc really began a revolution in legislative attitudes toward corrections. Texas was probably the toughest place to try to reform criminal justice, but Marc, working with capable legislative leaders and the Texas Public Policy Foundation, reworked the Texas criminal justice system, making intelligent choices about who should be incarcerated, holding those who are not a danger to society accountable in alternative ways. They put the savings from that into drug treatment and mental health treatment. They have been able to close six prisons so far, save five million dollars for the public, and dropped crime to its lowest point since 1967. It has been great for other states, because if Texas can do it, it can happen anywhere.

Grover Norquist is to my right, and is president of Americans for Tax Reform. We all know him for his leadership, literally changing the landscape politically with the tax pledge, and enforcing it, which is so important for credibility. Over ten years ago, Grover pulled aside and said, "Conservatives aren't doing enough about criminal justice reform." We have changed this, and he has been part of the effort, a driving force across the states, speaking to legislators, writing op-eds, doing radio shows, spreading the message that conservative principles give us a corrections system that costs less and protects us more. Grover, you have travelled the country, carrying the torch for this. I think it surprised us all how receptive conservative legislators are, especially in the Tea Party.

Julie Stewart, the founder and president of Families Against Mandatory Minimums has shown just how much one person can do. Her brother was convicted and received an absurdly long sentence. She did not know how that could be, and was willing to say, "This is wrong, this is against our liberty." She founded FAMM, after working at Cato before that, an institution we all love. She has put mandatory minimums on the map, and we now have strong bipartisan support to remove these one-size-fits-all sentences and instead tailoring it to the harm and culpability. Because of the drug war, everyone is affected by the criminal justice system. Julie has done a phenomenal job putting human faces on offenders doing long stretches of time.

Sam Brownback
Governor of Kansas

> SAM BROWNBACK *was sworn in as governor of Kansas on January 9, 2011. He served as Secretary of the Kansas Board of Agriculture from 1986-1993. During that time he also served as a White House Fellow in President George H. W. Bush's administration. In 1994, Kansans elected Brownback to the U.S. House of Representatives and, two years later, to the U.S. Senate seat once held by former Senator Bob Dole. In the Senate, Brownback was an effective advocate for Kansas interests while serving on the Appropriations Committee, the Agriculture Appropriations Subcommittee and the Homeland Security Subcommittee. He was a founding member of the Senate Fiscal Watch Team. Honoring his pledge to only serve two elected terms in the U.S. Senate, he did not seek reelection in 2010. As governor, Brownback is focused on growing the state's economy and increasing private sector jobs through improved regulations, controlled spending and lower tax rates. He has five measurable goals for his administration: Increase in net personal income; increase in private sector employment; increase in the percentage of 4th graders reading at grade level; increase in the percentage of high school graduates who are college or career ready; and decrease in the percentage of Kansas' children who live in poverty. Brownback and his wife, Mary, have five children, two of them are adopted. He graduated from Kansas State University in 1978 and the University of Kansas Law School in 1982.*

This is one of the issues that conservatives need to engage in. We have gotten too stuck in the mantra, you do the crime, you do the time. When I first ran in 1994 that was something that I used. The problem is that at some point, offenders are released, and we had sixty percent recidivism rates. Over time we began to engage a number of policies and proposals to get the recidivism rate down. Now we are down to about thirty percent, and trying to go further. I created the Second Chance Act, a bill designed to fund programs that cut recidivism rates by half over a five year time period.

At the end though, you have to work with the person that is there, and what their individual difficulty is. We have been engaging in mentoring programs. There needs to be a private mentor for everyone coming out of a Kansas prison. We release about six thousand, mostly men, a year. We have a little over four thousand private mentors. The first year recidivism rate was just under nine percent for those with a mentor. Without a mentor, the recidivism rate was twenty-one percent. It is important to find a good match, someone with a good heart that wants to do it. Often they are in the faith community. You need to find the match before the guy leaves prison, at least six months before he comes out, in order to build the relationship. These people cannot be pen pals, they need to be available twenty-four seven to help.

The second piece, that I think we have got a lot more work to do with, is the mental health arena. About thirty years ago, the country shut down all sorts of mental health hospitals, and the prisons ended up as mental institutions, which isn't working well. In Kansas, thirty-seven percent of adult men incarcerated have a mental illness. Including substance abuse, nearly sixty percent. We have started setting aside mental health wings, they've done this in Sedgwick County. We are taking people to halfway facilities that deal with mental health or substance abuse issues, because if someone has an issue, and you arrest him and put him in jail, he is not going to be better when you release him. Instead, you have exacerbated the situation. We are trying to put him in a situation that is less confrontational and that targets his problem.

Moving forward, I want to use welfare reform dollars to help people graduate from high school. That greatly reduces the likelihood of criminal behavior. We need to take welfare dollars, and really help people with personal coaches when they are in high school. We are getting a ninety-six percent graduation rate with that. We are also taking welfare dollars to increase our fourth grade reading levels. If you cannot read in fourth grade, you have a substantially higher likelihood of ending up in prison. This reduces public assistance and incarcerated populations later on.

Criminal justice reform and poverty reduction are two of the big, broader issues we need to engage in. Our solutions have worked, and we need to show that to the American public.

Grover Norquist
President, Americans for Tax Reform

> GROVER NORQUIST is is president of Americans for Tax Reform (ATR), a taxpayer advocacy group he founded in 1985 at President Reagan's request. ATR works to limit the size and cost of government and opposes higher taxes at the federal, state, and local levels and supports tax reform that moves towards taxing consumed income one time at one rate. ATR organizes the Taxpayer Protection Pledge, which asks all candidates for federal and state office to commit themselves in writing to the American people to oppose all tax increases. In the 114th Congress, 219 House members and 49 Senators have taken the pledge. On the state level, 14 governors and over 1,000 state legislators have taken the pledge. Norquist chairs the Washington, DC-based "Wednesday Meeting," a weekly gathering of more than 150 elected officials, political activists, and movement leaders. The meeting started in 1993 and takes place in ATR's conference room. There are now 60 similar "center-right" meetings in 48 states.

I cannot overemphasize the importance this issue has gained because of the success in Texas. When I testified in Florida, and said that they did this in Texas, people looked up. They want to know that it is not some Vermont idea. It had been done, and no one had lost an election over it. Elected officials need to know that something is safe. Convincing someone to try your great idea when it might cost them their career isn't a very good sales pitch. Telling people that this happened in Texas means that serious people have worked on it.

This is an issue with left/right agreement, which I want to make clear is very, very different from bipartisanship. Bipartisanship is usually the stupid party and the evil party getting together and doing something stupid and evil. Bipartisanship is when Republicans and Democrats get together and agree to raise their own pay and give themselves pensions. The present mess we have in each state, that is the result of bipartisanship. That is the seventy percent of the mushy middle. This, however, allows to have people on the right and people on the left—the ACLU, the NAACP—who have their own thoughts and reasons, making sure that this system destroys fewer lives, costs less money, and reduces crime.

The point is to drop crime in this country and to punish real criminals. Crime has been dropping in states that have reformed faster than in state that have not. You can save money, disrupt less lives, families, and communities. This is exactly where conservatives need to be. What took us so long? Well, I was working on all the things that government should not do. It was a good place to focus on. I figured that the wardens and prosecutors and generals were making sure that criminal justice and national defense were efficiently run. While we focused elsewhere, criminal justice became more and more expensive. When liberals brought up problems, we thought, "They're liberals—they're idiots—what do they know?" I credit the Christian effort, Chuck Colson and others, who focused on the people who went to prison. Two things happened when the fellowship went into the prisons. People began to focus on it, asking why it cost so much, and wanted to know how much it should cost. Now we have right/left coalitions for principled reasons. This is not about compromise. We are not sitting down with liberals and saying, "You don't want to punish criminals so we will punish them less." That is not it. We are realizing that this is the effective way to reduce crime, while doing less damage to individuals and taxpayers. People on the left have similar thoughts, sometimes for completely different reasons, but we can agree on some policies that move things forward. This brings the issue forward more quickly. We get attention because we are odd bedfellows. This is a good issue, a good set of reforms.

Only conservatives can talk about an issue and make elected officials feel comfortable doing something. They do not want to be attacked from the right if they decide that keeping seventy-five year old bank robbers in prison is a bad idea. They need to know that they will not be attacked from the right for being weak on crime. The Democrats need to know that this will not be used against them for being weak on crime. Conservative thought leaders and leftist thought leaders can talk to their own team and move this stuff forward.

Nothing is moving on other issues, so this is something where Rand Paul and Cory Booker can get together. Each Republican has a Democrat that they are working with. They are linked up, and we are seeing legislation move forward and take form. The last two years on the national, federal, level, and the last several years at the state level, we have had a tremendous opportunity for real progress. We are not deciding to not rearrest people; we do not need to rearrest them.

The press likes these issues; they cover them extensively. We can make sure that people are not attacked for reform.

Julie Stewart
President and Founder, Families Against Mandatory Minimums (FAMM)

> JULIE STEWART *is the president and founder of FAMM (Families Against Mandatory Minimums), a nonprofit, nonpartisan organization fighting for smart*

sentencing laws that maintain public safety. By putting a human face on mandatory sentencing laws, Julie Stewart and FAMM have played a major role in promoting sentencing reforms. FAMM's work has directly contributed to fairer sentences for an estimated 220,000 defendants and/or prisoners and has paved the way for a shift away from mandatory sentencing policies. Julie has testified many times before Congress and the U.S. Sentencing Commission about mandatory sentences and prison overcrowding. She has debated and discussed mandatory minimum sentences on numerous national television networks, including Fox News, ABC News, CBS News, CNN News, NBC News, PBS News, MTV, and on countless radio and local television programs throughout the country. In 2012, Julie appeared in The House I Live In, an award-winning documentary film about the drug war. Her work to reform mandatory sentencing laws has been honored with many awards including the Thomas Szasz Award for Outstanding Contributions to the Cause of Civil Liberties, the Champion of Justice Award from the National Association of Criminal Defense Attorneys, The Leadership for a Changing World award from the Ford Foundation, and the Citizen Activist Award from the Gleitsman Foundation. Julie graduated magna cum laude from Mills College in Oakland, California in 1988 with a bachelor's degree in International Relations.

Pat mentioned that I had a family member in prison. My brother was arrested for growing marijuana in Washington State in 1990, which is somewhat ironic since it is legal to do that now. He was growing marijuana in a garage in Washington, and he and his friends were arrested. Even though it was a relatively small case, it illustrates a lot of the problems that we have with mandatory minimums. The first is the fact that the case was a federal case. Where was the federal nexus? Why were they involved in the first place? This was in 1990, and as Governor Brownback says, "you do the crime, you do the time." But the question is, how much time? And who gets to decide?

That is one of the things that motivated me. I am not a lawyer, I am simply the sister of someone who was arrested and sentenced to prison for five years without parole for growing marijuana. At the time that he was sentenced, the judge said, "I do not want to give you this punishment, but I have no choice. My hands are tied by the laws Congress has passed." I was dumbstruck. I thought that federal judges had the power to deliver appropriate sentences. But mandatory minimums remove this discretion. Instead, legislators are making decisions about sentences for defendants that they have never laid eyes on. That is un-American. We are a country that values individualism. That is completely lost when someone is sentenced under mandatory minimums. My concern is that the escalation of punishments that we have seen as a result of the drug was has driven up all sentences. When mandatory drug sentences were passed in 1986, the average sentence for federal sentencing was four years. Today, it is nine and a half years. Today, the average drug offender is not more than twice as dangerous as he or she was in 1986.

What have we gotten for that amount of overincarceration? There are enormous budget deficits in states across the country. Although crime has dropped, crime has dropped in states that have reduced their prison populations at the same time. Both conservative and liberals have thought in past years that if you put more people in prison, you will reduce crime. I agree, if we locked up everyone in America, we would not have much crime. There is a cost benefit that must be weighed, and we have gone past the tipping point long ago. We need to ask, how much time is enough?

I spoke to someone yesterday, a federal drug offender, incarcerated for fifteen years on his third offense. He was sentenced as a career criminal. His priors were ridiculous. They were all small amounts of drugs. His second offence was thirty-four grams of marijuana. That is thirty-four Sweet and Low packages. His last conviction was for growing two hundred and fifty marijuana plants. Then the case went federal. On the surface, you might think, "Oh my goodness, a career criminal! We want him off the streets!" He ran a pizza shop in Kentucky. He supports a wife and a brand new baby. His father, eighty-four years old, writes me handwritten notes, asking me to please help his son, telling me that they need him at home. He has done five years. His father will be dead before he gets out. What good is this sentence doing? What good is being served by his incarceration? He could leave, support his family, he could get back into business.

Almost everyone who goes to prison comes back out eventually, so recidivism is a huge issue. We have to be prepared to help them re-enter society. There are so many ridiculous barriers. When my brother was released, he wanted to be a realtor. He went through all of the classes, but was denied a license because he had a felony record. How is that helping him become a law-abiding citizen? I urge you, think about these issues. Think about people that need second chances. My brother agreed that he needed to be arrested, that he needed to get his act together. But how much time did he need for that? And who should decide?

Marc Levin

Director, Center for Effective Justice, Texas Public Policy Foundation
Policy Director, Right on Crime

MARC A. LEVIN *is a director of the Center for Effective Justice at the Texas Public Policy Foundation. Levin is an attorney and an accomplished author on legal and public policy issues. Levin has served as a law clerk to Judge Will Garwood on the U.S. Court of Appeals for the Fifth Circuit and Staff Attorney at the Texas Supreme Court. In 1999, he graduated with honors from the University of Texas with a B.A. in Plan II Honors and Government. In 2002, Levin received his J.D. with honors from the University of Texas School of Law. Levin's articles on law and public policy have been featured in publications such as the Wall Street Journal, USA Today, Texas Review of Law & Politics, National Law Journal, New York Daily News, Jerusalem Post, Toronto Star, Atlanta Journal-Constitution, Philadelphia Inquirer, San Francisco Chronicle, Washington Times, Los Angeles Daily Journal, Charlotte Observer, Dallas Morning News, Houston Chronicle, Austin American-Statesman, San Antonio Express-News and Reason Magazine.*

In Texas, Right on Crime served as a basis to take to other states what we had done in Texas. In 2007 we were looking at a projected growth of seventeen thousand over five years. We would need to add seventeen thousand prison beds onto a hundred and fifty-five thousand. We computed the cost of building and operating those beds as over two billion dollars over five years. Instead we set up an alternative plan, more drug courts, risk assessments, and stronger probation. As Pat said, our crime rate has is the lowest it has been since 1967. That has given us the credibility to go to other states and persuade them to follow our example.

Conservative governors have been the ones stepping up the plate and leading the charge. To give you a few examples, Governor Deal in Georgia has presided over three straight, really significant adult and juvenile justice reform packages. In the most recent elected he campaigned on it. He sent out mailings about the drop in crime and incarceration. He won on stronger margins and received stronger votes in areas that do not traditionally vote Republican. Governor Kasich campaigned on this as well in the last election. When we began, we had to convince officials that this would not lose them elections, but now they use it to help keep their jobs.

To give you other examples, in Mississippi, Governor Phil Bryant presided over a very successful package. He announced before the legislative session, "I want to bring Right on Crime to Mississippi." South Carolina is a great story as well. In 2010, they passed a comprehensive reform package, reduced penalties for low-level drug possession, and actually increased penalties for crimes that were violent but weren't properly classified. They also made sure that people released had supervision. They were not max-ing out of their sentences. They used risk assessment to ensure that people are on the right level of supervision when they are on probation. Their crime rate is down seventeen percent and their incarceration rate is down fourteen percent.

One issue that hasn't come up today is the victims of crime. We need to get restitution to someone who was victimized. It is important to realize that people on probation pay ninety-six times more in restitution than someone in prison. Obviously sometimes someone needs to be prison, but today we have a system that allows the government to take the first cut of fines and fees from people with little money and the victim is the last in line to get restitution. That is wrong. We need to realize that the individual is the victim of a crime, not the government.

I'd also like to touch on our work in Overcriminalization. We have a reception coming up, I hope you all got an invitation to the Right on Crime oyster reception, it is themed with the eleven felonies that we have in relating to oyster harvesting. This is a problem throughout the country. At the federal level the congressional research office counted over forty-five hundred federal crimes before giving up. That doesn't even begin to cover the regulatory crimes created by federal and state agencies every day of the week. We need to get rid of the ridiculous delegation of power from our elected officials to unelected bureaucrats.

There is still so much we need to do on this issue. It is truly conservatives who have the credibility on this issue. Before Right on Crime, there were people on the left saying that society caused crime, not individuals, and people on the right were saying that everyone should be locked up, not caring about the cost. That doesn't hold true to limited government or the principles that we hold dear. Our course embodies conservative principles.

One of the reasons that we have seen a shift is that the Tea Party has an inherent skepticism of government that the "mushy middle" does not have. There are some people on the libertarian life, like the ACLU, who have skepticism about government in things like wrongful convictions. Michael Morton in Texas, for example, who was held wrongfully for thirty years after prosecutors obstructed DNA testing. Conservatives are now applying the same skepticism that they have had for years on agencies such as education and healthcare, to criminal justice and corrections. Maryland is an interesting example. They passed an earned credits bill that allowed people to earn time off their probation. If they paid their restitution, got a degree, held a job, these things that reduced their likelihood of recidivism, they could earn time. Unfortunately, moderates on both sides in Maryland were the ones that ultimately defeated the bill.

Q&A

JULIE STEWART: In Michigan in 1998, Governor Engler signed a bill to eliminate the life sentence for fist offenders possessing 650 grams of cocaine or heroin. He received no blowback for that. The Republican legislature got no blowback for that and it was 1998. In this past year in Florida, Governor Rick Scott signed a bill to change the gun mandatory sentencing laws as well as some prescription pill mandatory sentencing laws. Republicans have been incredibly helpful in this area.

GOVERNOR BROWNBACK: It is important to consider law enforcement in this discussion. It is a hard profession to hire people into, we are spending money and upping pay to get people. We need to provide protection to law enforcement. We need to consider what is effective, and I do not know that these conversations are happening.

QUESTION: I would like to know how much is being spent incarcerating people who are here illegally?

PAT NOLAN: Well, as far as I know, Congress hasn't been able to get those figures.

QUESTION: Governor, you mentioned mentoring programs. Are these people compensated, or are they volunteers?

GOVERNOR BROWNBACK: All volunteers.

JULIE STEWART: We should be considered mandatory minimums for gun sentences as well. They are awful. Many of them only require the gun to be in the room, you can be doing something completely unrelated to its presence. We hope that will be an issue that legislative bodies are willing to look at. We had great success in Florida last year.

MARC LEVIN: I'd also like to address limitations on employment. Our view is that it is not the role of government to tell private businesses what can be their job criteria. However, in Texas, our solution is non-disclosure. It is short of an expunction, for non-violent offenses for which you have received deferred adjudication.

The government created these records to begin with, now we are saying that they should be able to prove themselves law-abiding. Then they can be granted the order, and prosecutors can see past it, law enforcement can see past it, but you can say on a form that you have not been convicted of an offense.

PAT NOLAN: I dissent a little from that. I agree that jobs are essential to getting these people back on their feet. On the other hand, that can be valuable information for an employer. I think that the solution is the free market. Some employers take the box off the application, review your qualifications, and then can ask in an interview. Then they can really evaluate the risk, without compromising their evaluation of you.

It would be better if more employers did that. One galvanizing plant in Pennsylvania began hiring ex-offenders for faith-based reasons, but after trying it, they now have a standing offer with the local prison, because they are good hires. Over half of his employees are ex-offenders.

QUESTION: I think that the mentoring program is a great idea. Some people believe that social programs will fix this situation in twenty years, but people are dying now. I am running for state senate in Virginia, and I could use your help and suggestions about that mentoring program in Kansas.

MARC LEVIN: We also need to address the employer liability for hiring ex-offenders. There is a bill this session to protect landlords form being sued simply because they rented to an ex-offender. There are exceptions for rapists and things like that. We ought to focus on things that prevent people from getting ahead. The voting issue is more of a political question. This isn't an issue that Right on Crime has addressed.

PAT NOLAN: It may be much ado about a very small few, but when a judge puts the hammer down, you are banished. At some point, when you have paid your debt, done you time, finished probation or parole, you should eventually be accepted back. I think there is a concern that there will be a horde of ex-felons voting en bloc for liberal Democrats. I was in prison for twenty-nine months. In prison, they like to watch cop shows, and they root for the cops. The death penalty would pass overwhelmingly in prison. They know the characters that are being dealt with. I do not think the harm is really there, but I see a great good in bringing people back into the body politic.

Texas Prison Reform 2.0

SEN. JOAN HUFFMAN | SEN. JOHN WHITMIRE | REP. TAN PARKER
BILL MONTGOMERY | ADAM GELB
MODERATOR: **MARC LEVIN**

Texas continues to attract positive national attention for closing prisons while achieving its lowest crime rate since 1968. However, as the state continues to grow, policymakers must build on this success to take the steps to further enhance public safety, empower victims, control costs, and reform offenders. Learn how this can be accomplished in the upcoming legislative session.

This event took place at Texas Public Policy Foundation's 2015 Policy Orientation.

Marc Levin
Director, Center for Effective Justice, Texas Public Policy Foundation
Policy Director, Right on Crime

> MARC A. LEVIN *is a director of the Center for Effective Justice at the Texas Public Policy Foundation. Levin is an attorney and an accomplished author on legal and public policy issues. Levin has served as a law clerk to Judge Will Garwood on the U.S. Court of Appeals for the Fifth Circuit and Staff Attorney at the Texas Supreme Court. In 1999, he graduated with honors from the University of Texas with a B.A. in Plan II Honors and Government. In 2002, Levin received his J.D. with honors from the University of Texas School of Law. Levin's articles on law and public policy have been featured in publications such as the Wall Street Journal, USA Today, Texas Review of Law & Politics, National Law Journal, New York Daily News, Jerusalem Post, Toronto Star, Atlanta Journal-Constitution, Philadelphia Inquirer, San Francisco Chronicle, Washington Times, Los Angeles Daily Journal, Charlotte Observer, Dallas Morning News, Houston Chronicle, Austin American-Statesman, San Antonio Express-News and Reason Magazine.*

I am Marc Levin, the Director for the Center for Effective Justice at the Texas Public Policy Foundation and the Policy Director for our Right on Crime initiative. We have a tremendous selection of speakers, and we will have Q and A as always. We have had a tremendous run of success in Texas with adult corrections reform. The crime rate in Texas is down by more that 22 percent over the last several years. Simultaneously our incarceration rate has dropped by 12 percent. There are many innovations across counties in Texas and a growing consensus that we need to take the next step. We need to continue to ensure that we defend the gains achieved by prioritizing the proven alternatives to incarceration, such as drug courts, treatment programs, and specialty courts. The next legislative session holds great promise for us to continue the great progress that we have seen. The expertise we gain today will help us to do that.

Adam Gelb

Director, Public Safety Performance Project, The Pew Charitable Trust

ADAM GELB *directs Pew's public safety performance project, which helps states advance policies and practices in adult and juvenile sentencing and corrections that protect public safety, hold offenders accountable, and control corrections costs. As the project lead, Gelb oversees Pew's assistance to states seeking a greater public safety return on their corrections spending. He also supervises a vigorous research portfolio that highlights strategies for reducing recidivism while cutting costs. Gelb speaks frequently with the media about national trends and state innovations, and regularly advises policy makers on implementation of practical, cost-effective policies. Gelb has been involved in crime control and prevention issues for the past 25 years as a journalist, congressional aide, and senior state government official. He began his career as a reporter at the Atlanta Journal-Constitution and staffed the U.S. Senate Judiciary Committee during negotiations and final passage of the Violent Crime Control and Law Enforcement Act of 1994. From 1995 to 2000, as policy director for the lieutenant governor of Maryland, Gelb was instrumental in developing several nationally recognized anti-crime initiatives. He served as executive director of the Georgia Sentencing Commission from 2001 to 2003. Before joining Pew, he was vice president for programs at the Georgia Council on Substance Abuse. Gelb graduated from the University of Virginia and holds a master's degree from Harvard University's Kennedy School of Government.*

For fifty years the incarceration rate was the same. Criminologists refer to this as stable punishment. We had an explosion starting in the 1970s and it continued through the 1980s and 90s and into this century really until 2008. We had one in every one hundred adults in this country behind bars. Including the prison and jail populations, there were 2.3 million people behind bars.

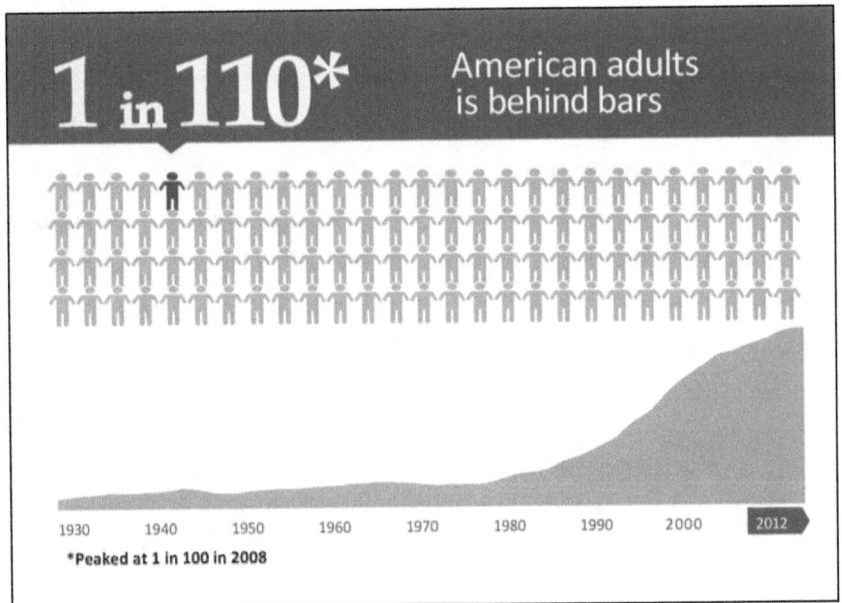

Today, at the year-end of 2012, the numbers have fallen back. That is in good part due to the efforts here in Texas and in other states. Even if the prison population has not dropped, it still has not risen with the population. Looking at probation and parole, there is a similar trend. It peaked in 2008 at one in thirty-one adults under correctional control.

Three percent of the adult population is in prison or jail, or on probation or parole. That has also dropped. The most recent numbers form the Bureau of Justice Statistics at the end of 2013 that it is one in thirty-five. That is still incredibly high, but it is moving in the right direction. It shows limited government, and fiscal discipline. The funding has not dipped yet, but it has flattened out.

Here is a map showing the states that have participated in the Justice Reinvestment Initiative. We do not have every state here that has done reforms. The Justice Reinvestment program is an intensive technical assistance model that Pew, the Justice Department, the Council of State Governments Justice Center, and others have participated in to assist states in analyzing their prison population in order to determine what is driving them higher and what can be done to bend that curve, consistent with public safety. About thirty or thirty-one states have been through this process. Several have made substantial gains, shown in blue. Gains mean that they have passed significant reforms in sentencing and release policies, as well as reentry and other programs that reduce recidivism. The states in yellow have more limited reforms. Alabama, Nebraska, Utah, and Washington are actively working on this initiative in their 2015 sessions.

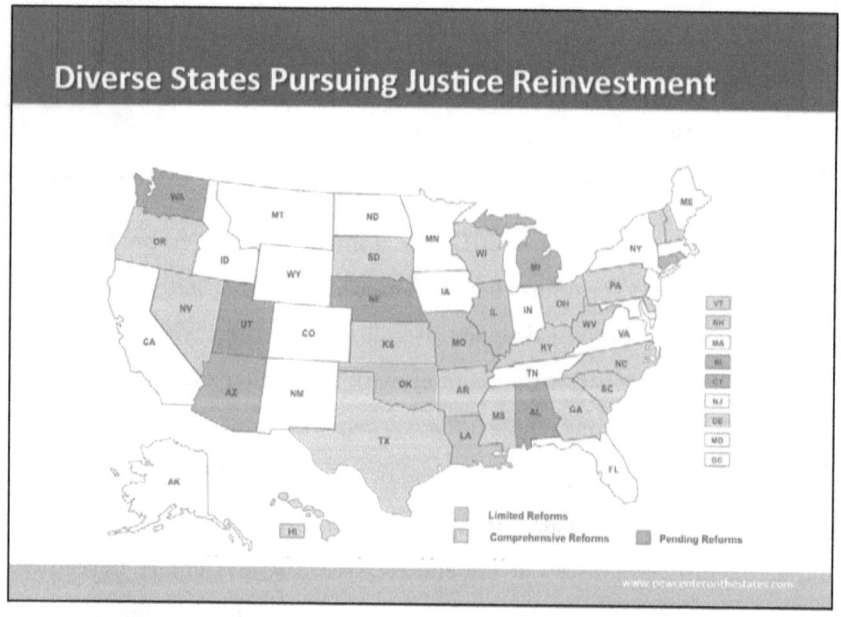

If you notice the chart you see that as time goes on, the reforms increase and become more broad. It is important to ask why this is happening.

There is an assumption that budget cuts are the reason that sentencing reform has been happening. States, unlike the federal government, have to make ends meet. They have to balance their budgets. When the recession hit, states started to make a lot of changes, some that they did not like in order to balance their budgets. From our vantage point at Pew, there is no doubt that dollars are part of the equation. Dollars get people to the table, but they do not result in votes. There are not unanimous votes for reforms that states are opposed to on principle.

> **Why?**
>
> **1** **State Successes in Reducing Crime and Incarceration**
>
> **2** **Supportive Political Environment**
>
> **3** **Credible Alternatives**
>
> www.pewcenteronthestates.com

In Texas the reforms happened in 2005 and 2007, when the budget was still looking good. Texas is Exhibit A, showing that money is not the driving force. Now that Texas has such as successful track record, states are starting to see that it is possible to put the brakes on prison growth and reduce crime simultaneously. There is a supportive political environment, particularly with leading conservatives around the country. TPPF and Right on Crime have helped organize this. Policy makers are starting to recognize and see the research on approaches that are more effective and less expensive than prison. We know what works now. Nothing is foolproof, but there is good research. This is driving the changes around the country.

Here are examples of two of the reforms that we have seen. In California, Proposition 47 was enacted to change sentencing for property and drug crimes. It was a big ballot measure. There were millions and millions of dollars spent on advocacy and it was estimated to save about five or six thousand beds a year. California went about reform differently in 2009, similar to Texas, as far as incentivizing decisions to revoke people from probation. In 2009 California adopted a Performance Incentive Funding Program. They seceded forty-five million dollars to the California counties for probation. This was invested in evidence-based program and helped the counties reduce probation failure by 23 percent. In the last four years this has led to a reduction in prison admissions by over twenty-seven thousand offenders, and saving the state up to 920 million dollars. Counties were reimbursed as half of that money was ploughed back into supervision. This was a win-win for California that had no ballot initiative or millions spent on advocacy. Mississippi has also made extensive reforms this past legislative session. This has saved Mississippi a quarter billion dollars.

The last message is the notion that Texas is really demonstrating soundly and that it is not a zero sum game between crime and imprisonment. The assumption that if you want crime to keep going down, prisons have to keep going up is just not being borne out in the last several years. In fact, the states where imprisonment is dropping, the crime rate is dropping faster than in the states where the imprisonment rate is still rising. Comparing Texas with Nebraska, you see from 2008 to 2013, the imprisonment rate and the crime rate dropping double digits in Texas whereas in Nebraska, the imprisonment rate continues to climb, with the crime decline even less here than in Texas.

So congratulations again to Senator Whitmire, Representative Madden, who works now with TPPF as a senior fellow on the Right On Crime, to the example that Texas continues to provide across the country and to the other leaders here as well. The Texas story is obviously saving a tremendous amount of money and improving public safety in the state, as well as driving a tremendous amount of the conversation around the country. You all should be really proud of what you've accomplished.

Sentencing and Corrections Reforms in Justice Reinvestment States

Policy Reform	2014		2013			2012					2011					2010			2009			2008				2007			Total
	ID	MS	OR	SD	WV	KS	MO	DE	GA	PA	HI	OK	AR	KY	AL	LA	NC	OH	SC	NH	MI	IL	WI	AZ	PA	CT	RI	VT	KS	NV	TX	
Sentencing/Pretrial																																
Reclassify/reduce drug offenses	✓	✓	✓	✓																												8
Reclassify/reduce property offenses	✓	✓	✓	✓									✓																			7
Establish/expand presumptive probation for certain offenses							✓	✓	✓							✓			✓											✓		7
Revise sentencing enhancements													✓	✓														✓		✓		5
Revise mandatory minimums								✓					✓	✓				✓													✓	5
Reduce crack-powder cocaine disparity																										✓						2
Revise sentencing guidelines/establish sentencing commission										✓												✓									✓	3
Improve pretrial release system													✓					✓					✓						✓			4
Establish presentence assessment												✓													✓				✓	✓	✓	6
Revise drug-free school zone																																2
Authorize reincarceration sentencing											✓											✓						✓				3
Release																																
Revise parole hearing/decision/eligibility standards						✓	✓					✓		✓			✓	✓	✓	✓	✓	✓	✓			✓	✓	✓				12
Expand good-time/reduce prison credits (Re-entry) leave						✓	✓							✓		✓	✓	✓	✓	✓	✓	✓				✓			✓			12
Establish/expand geriatric or medical parole																									✓			✓				5
Community Corrections																																
Establish earned discharge (probation/parole)			✓						✓				✓			✓	✓	✓	✓	✓	✓	✓						✓	✓	✓		12
Authorize performance incentive funding																		✓		✓	✓	✓						✓	✓	✓		8
Authorize administrative jail sanctions									✓		✓			✓			✓	✓		✓								✓	✓	✓	✓	11
Authorize graduated responses for violations		✓	✓	✓					✓	✓		✓		✓			✓	✓		✓	✓	✓						✓	✓	✓		15
Cap revocation time									✓					✓			✓	✓	✓	✓	✓	✓						✓		✓		10
Establish/improve electronic monitoring														✓				✓		✓							✓	✓		✓	✓	7
Establish mandatory reentry supervision					✓			✓					✓	✓				✓							✓			✓	✓			8
Require/improve risk-needs assessment		✓		✓	✓	✓		✓	✓		✓	✓		✓			✓	✓		✓	✓	✓						✓	✓	✓		17
Require evidence-based practices				✓					✓								✓	✓		✓	✓	✓	✓						✓	✓	✓	11
Reform/pilot specialty courts (HOPE, drug courts, etc.)			✓			✓			✓							✓		✓			✓								✓	✓	✓	9
Reduce probation terms																						✓										2
Improve interventions such as sub abuse/mental health/CBT		✓		✓				✓	✓	✓		✓		✓			✓	✓	✓	✓	✓							✓	✓	✓	✓	14
Sustainability																																
Require fiscal impact statements																		✓	✓	✓									✓	✓	✓	6
Establish leadership/board qualification requirements																		✓	✓					✓						✓		4
Require data collection/performance measurement		✓	✓	✓	✓	✓		✓	✓			✓		✓			✓	✓	✓	✓	✓	✓		✓				✓	✓	✓		17
Establish measures to streamline/improve efficiency of system		✓	✓	✓					✓					✓			✓	✓	✓	✓	✓	✓							✓	✓	✓	12
Improve restitution/victim notification systems		✓	✓											✓							✓								✓	✓	✓	6
Establish oversight council																				✓												

Bill Montgomery

Maricopa County Attorney, Gilbert, Arizona

BILL MONTGOMERY *was first elected Maricopa County Attorney in a Special Election in 2010 and re-elected in 2012 on a pledge to fight crime, honor victims' rights, and protect and strengthen our community. As a West Point Graduate, decorated Gulf War Veteran, professional prosecutor and former Deputy County Attorney, he has dedicated his personal and professional life to serving others. As County Attorney, Bill is committed to vigorously prosecuting crimes and holding criminals accountable and believes in the responsible application of Arizona's tough sentencing laws to ensure violent and repeat criminals are kept from our fellow citizens and communities. He is committed to partnering with law enforcement along with business and civic leaders to protect and strengthen our communities, and strongly supports the involvement of local law enforcement in assisting with enforcement of our immigration laws. Recognizing that violent child sexual predators cannot be rehabilitated, Bill has been an outspoken advocate for life sentences for these offenders. He also supports GPS monitoring for other convicted child molesters, and Internet sting operations to capture child predators before they get the chance to victimize children. His goal is to let would-be child predators know they will find no safe haven in Arizona. Bill is equally determined to fight fraud and identity theft through the County Attorney's specialized Fraud and Identity Theft Enforcement bureau. He also supports the Castle Doctrine Law, which recognizes a citizen's right to defend his or her family without fear of prosecution; and Arizona's Three Strikes Law, which targets repeat violent criminals. Bill has helped shape legislation designed to protect victims of crime and reform Child Protective Services, and he continues to be a passionate advocate for Victims Rights in Arizona as Maricopa County Attorney. Bill currently resides in Gilbert, Arizona with his wife and their children.*

I want to give a brief overview of my jurisdiction and some of the issues that we face there. If you're going to talk about incarceration rates and criminal justice policy, it's important to understand the factors that go into the type of crime committed there and what those states have to deal with in carrying out the responsibilities to ensure that their citizens are safe and their liberties are protected.

In Arizona, we have a bit of a unique environment, though we share some similarities with Texas. Maricopa County is the fourth most populous county in the nation, with four million people. Phoenix, the state capital, is within my jurisdiction. It's the sixth largest city, and is where my main office is located. Maricopa County has two-thirds of the state's population and about two-thirds of the crime. Therefore, we are the largest contributor to our state's prison population. Our prison system is known as the Department of Corrections (DOC). The county itself is the fifteenth largest county in the country, bigger than some east coast states at 9,200 square miles. My office is the third largest county-based prosecution agency in the country with over 320 prosecutors. I also have a civil responsibility, where the remainder of the attorneys come from. In last calendar year, we prosecuted over 31,000 felony cases and about another twenty-six thousand misdemeanors. We do have responsibility in some limited jurisdiction courts within the county.

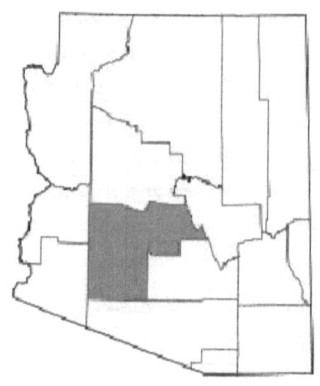

We are a destination county for human and drug smuggling from Mexico. The southern border for Arizona is made up of the Yuma and Tucson sectors. For calendar year 2014, the Tucson sector was the site of roughly half of all drugs smuggled in the United States. We were number two for human smuggling. There have been years where we were also the location where half of all human beings were smuggled, but the Rio Grande sector is now outpacing us by a factor of about three. That's not a race we want to win, but it's not a situation that's acceptable either. Within my county, we have command and control of all elements of the Sinaloa Cartel because we are the distribution hub for their heroin distribution network throughout the United States. This is what we get to deal with. I want you to keep that in mind when I talk to you about how Arizona uses incarceration as a tool for public safety.

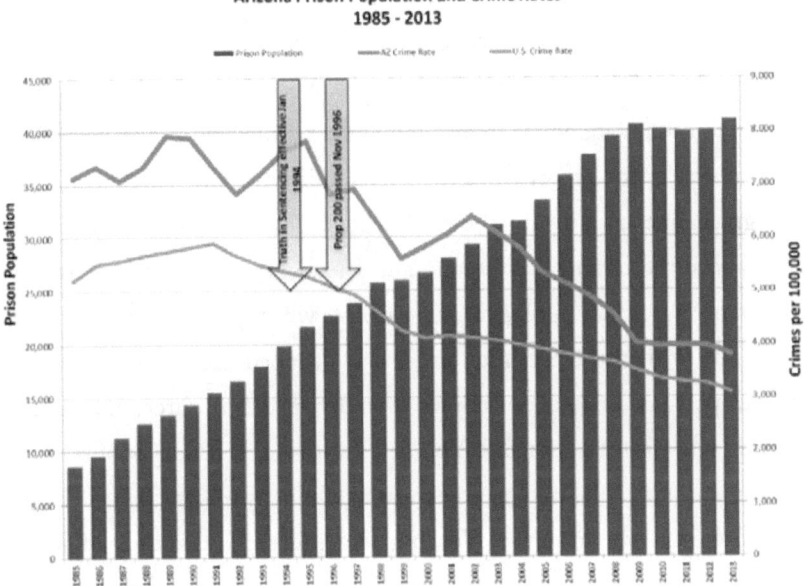

This chart right here shows, from 1985 until 2013, our prison population growth based upon total population at the end of each year. Our commitment rates from month to month and year to year may differ, but this is what the growth has been. For the most recent year, in 2013, as reflected on the chart, we were in excess of forty thousand people. The arrow on the left indicates when Truth In Sentencing went into effect in Arizona, in 1994. That law requires inmates sent to the Department of Corrections, who have not committed a specific type of offenses that require flat time, must serve eighty-five percent of that sentence. The arrow to the right highlights 1996, when Arizona voters passed a change to our probation statutes that mandates substance abuse treatment for the first two drug possession or use offenses. Over this same timeframe, the incarceration rate in Arizona has increased about eighteen to nineteen percent while our population has increased about fifty-four percent. Within the last ten to fifteen years, Arizona has been in the top three, at least in some years dropped down maybe to the top five, for fastest growing states. My county has been in the top ten among the fastest growing counties in the nation, leading up to about 2007. We're slowly inching our way back up now. The red line is our state's crime rate, made up of both violent crime and property crimes in the part one crime report from the FBI's uniform crime reporting system. The green line underneath shows the same type of crimes nationally. So we're above the national crime rate and I have already told you why. Over that same timeframe, going back to 2002, when you compare Arizona's crime rate with the US crime rate, it has dropped precipitously. In some areas of part one crimes, our crimes have dropped two, three, and as much as four times faster nationally. You can see that our prison population increased and our DOC budget is requesting almost a billion dollars. That's a whole lot of people in prison. Yes, but remember, the first duty of government is to protect public safety. Every dollar spent by government on public safety is a constitutional dollar, versus a feel good program or something that somebody may want to take credit for in order to get reelected. This is something that government is supposed to do.

The next couple of slides are statistics from a report done back in 2009, published in the beginning of 2010 by Dr. Darrell Fisher, the former statistician for the Department of Corrections for the Arizona Prosecuting Attorney's Advisory Council, made up of elected prosecutors, some municipal prosecutors and our attorney general. The council wanted to know, "Who's in prison?" We keep hearing there are too many people in prison. If we have the most violent and those most responsible for committing felonies in prison, then we can say that's who should be in prison. If you want to let people out, we want to be able to identify specifically which category of crime or which profile of offender do you want to release? This study from 2009 was repeated again in 2011 and 2013. The numbers are somewhat similarly reflective of what I'm going to show you in this initial study. This now allows us to talk about our prison population and who are we spending those dollars on incarcerating, from an objective, data driven standpoint.

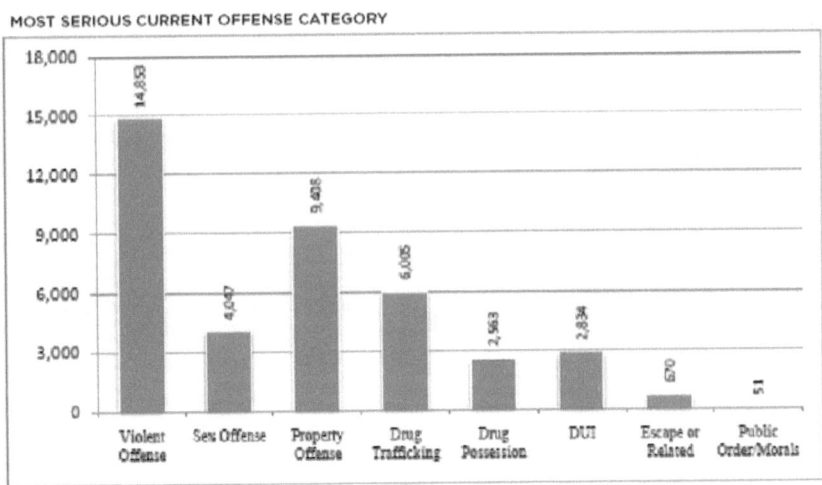

In our first graph, we'll show you that for violent offenses, the most serious current offense category, easily outpaces all other commitments. The next ones, are for sex offenses, then property offenses and then drug trafficking. These offenses are high because we're the main thoroughfare for the Mexican cartels to push their product up through the United States. Thanks to Colorado and their legalization efforts and the federal government's ineffective or indifferent attitude, those cartels are now trying to get to Colorado.

Now over this same timeframe, we did see a tremendous drop or flattening out of our prison population for the first time in the history of Arizona. What we found in the course of those additional studies is that we were revoking fewer people to prison from probation, and fewer low level felons or non-violent felons were going to prison. We were utilizing diversion and offering substance abuse treatment programs. At the same time however, our violent and repeat felons started to increase.

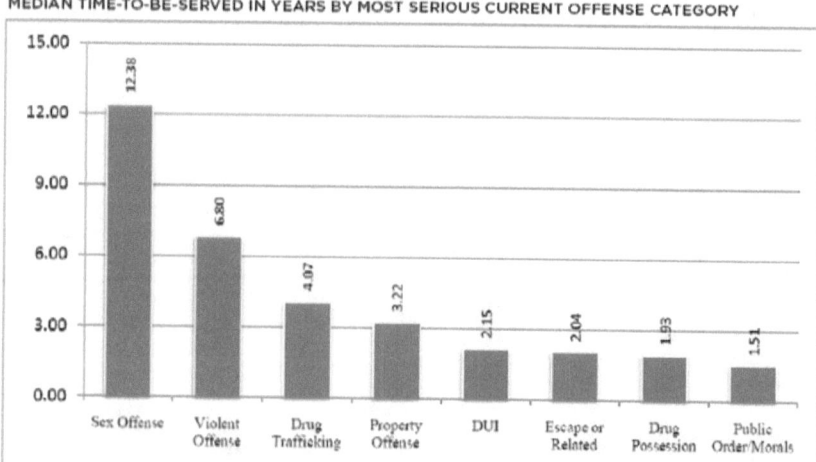

MEDIAN TIME-TO-BE-SERVED IN YEARS BY MOST SERIOUS CURRENT OFFENSE CATEGORY

This next slide is the median time to be served in years by the most serious, current offense category. I mention this because one of the things you need to keep in mind when we talk about the incarceration rate in the United States or in any given state is that for the most part it's a transitory population. These are people that are coming in for a few years and then going out, and in terms of the US incarceration rate, that includes our jails. Other countries around the world don't have a jail type system. We also incarcerate our seriously mentally ill. That's a topic for another day. Other countries won't incarcerate, they'll put them in a hospital setting, but it's still a restriction on their liberty. They get to call it something different when they're reporting that information to the UN. Plus, I really don't think we can count on Cuba, Iran, China, or other totalitarian regimes to be honest about who they're incarcerating.

Some of the criticisms of the 2009 report we commissioned have been that prosecutors got what prosecutors paid for. Prosecutors cannot create a criminal history where it does not exist. Prosecutors cannot say someone's in prison for ten years for an offense they were not convicted of and were not sentenced for. Again, in the median total time to be served by most serious current offense, I picked the top ten. The top ten people and their median total time to be served in prison in Arizona in 2009, which includes first degree murder, second degree murder, dangerous or deadly assault by a prisoner or juvenile, sexual conduct with a minor, continuous sexual abuse of a child, sexual assault, molestation of a child, manslaughter, sexual exploitation of a minor, and a prisoner committed an assault with intent to incite a riot or participate in a riot. Who do you want to let out? Who do you want to have move in next door to you? Who do you think letting out would contribute to public safety? This is what this report has allowed us to focus on. When we look at this now as prosecutors and share this information with our legislators and with folks in the public, we can say who we're incarcerating is who you want us to be incarcerating.

NUMBER OF PRIOR FELONIES

Number of Prior Felonies	Inmates #	%
None	6,535	16.2%
One	11,257	27.8%
Two	5,738	14.2%
Three	4,435	11.0%
Four	3,417	8.5%
Five	2,566	6.3%
Six	1,813	4.5%
Seven	1,407	3.5%
Eight	964	2.4%
Nine	615	1.5%
Ten or More	1,684	4.2%
Grand Total	**40,431**	**100.0%**
Two or More	22,639	56.0%
Three or More	16,901	41.8%

Next, this shows for those who have been committed to prison, how many prior felonies they have committed. The top line where it says none, the only way to go to prison in Arizona without having a prior felony criminal history is you have to commit a certain series of offenses - a dangerous crime against a child, molestation of a child, sexual misconduct with a child, or certain dangerous offenses like deadly weapon or a dangerous instrument or serious physical injury. 56 percent of those in prison had two or more. 41 percent, 42 percent had three or more felonies. During that same time in the Truth in Sentencing, we found that the average sentence was about .3 years longer than what it had been before Truth in Sentencing. We took a look at for all those offenders who had been sentenced in that .3 year extra timeframe and focused on what we did deterrence-wise. We prevented 7500 felonies and this breaks out of each category. We prevented those offenses by increasing those sentences. Over the entire time for those who had been sentenced under Truth in Sentencing, we prevented one million crimes. Why is that important? You have to look at the other side of that ledger. Sure, there is a cost for incarceration, but there's also savings. There's savings in the figure of the amount of money that gets spent by the victim of crime who's out of work, has to go get health care, and otherwise has to take time off work to show up in court. Those offenses averaged five hundred bucks each which totals five hundred million dollars, making savings of half a billion dollars in those fifteen years in costs to our fellow citizens.

Since Truth in Sentencing, 220,499 Offenders Sentenced and the following crimes were not committed during the .3 year period of increased incarceration:

7,514 Felonies precluded:
- 1,674 Drug Possession Offenses
- 746 Burglaries
- 657 Motor Vehicle Thefts
- 638 DUIs
- 620 Aggravated Assaults
- 462 Drug Trafficking Cases
- 435 Weapons Offenses
- 426 Forgery/Counterfeiting/ID Theft
- 350 Larceny/Thefts
- 293 Robberies
- 176 other Assaults
- 117 Property Theft cases
- 112 Fraud/Embezzlement
- 83 Vandalism
- 68 Domestic Violence Offenses against families and children
- 61 Murder/Non-Negligent Homicides
- 54 Sex Offenses
- 20 Forcible Rapes
- 8 Prostitution/Commercial Vice
- 7 Arsons
- 2 Negligent Manslaughters
- 505 Miscellaneous Offenses

** - **Overall, from 1995 to 2010, total estimated crimes prevented through incapacitation = 1 million**

I will next look at states that have truth in sentencing versus states without it. In just about every category measurement, states that have truth-in-sentencing laws have seen greater reductions in crime from 1991 to 2010. This slide will show that in the three different periods that we used in this study, initially 94.2 percent were in prison for a violent or repeat felony. The non-violent offender category includes child molesters, so it is important to be careful with these distinctions. However, over these three studies, we have seen our violent population went up 4.3 percent while the non-violent offenders dropped 5.25 percent.

PERCENTAGE DECLINES IN CRIME RATES (1991-2010)
- All Reported Crime: TIS (-44.6%); Non-TIS (-39.3%)
- Violent Crime: TIS (-49.1%); Non-TIS (-37.7%)
- Property Crime: TIS (-43.9%); Non-TIS (-39.5%)
- Murder/Non-Negligent Manslaughter: TIS (-50.6%); Non-TIS (-53.1%)
- Forcible Rape: TIS (-37.9%); Non-TIS (-26.9%)
- Robbery: TIS (-58.7%); Non-TIS (-43.8%)
- Aggravated Assault: TIS (-43.7%); Non-TIS States (-35.7%)
- Burglary: TIS (-45.1%); Non-TIS (-41.3%)
- Larceny-Theft: TIS (-39.1%); Non-TIS (-34.7%)
- Motor Vehicle Theft: TIS (-64.2%); Non-TIS (-62.0%)

Now I will discuss what we are doing to limit those entering prison. We are encouraging people to undergo substance abuse treatment. If you successfully complete a diversion, you can avoid having a felony conviction. We use a drug court that has a successful record in limiting offender incarceration. Here are some numbers that indicate the successful diversion for fiscal year 2014. 86 percent successfully completed that program. That is over twenty-one hundred people who will not go through my office to be prosecuted. Over sixty-one thousand who have gone through the drug diversion program, and the overwhelming majority of those in the lifetime, seventy-five percent successful, we have not had to prosecute them.

We use a determinate sentencing structure. This only constrains the judges that would need help. In each of these different categories, we are looking at the type of offense that was committed, the criminal history, and the circumstances, both mitigating and aggravating. Judges are able to move within those ranges, as a fact finder.

SUBSTANCE ABUSE ISSUES AND DRUG POSSESSION/USE OFFENSES

<u>Voter Initiative November 1996</u>
  First 2 Offenses Mandatory Substance Abuse Treatment
    1st Offense – No incarceration imposed
    2nd Offense – No prison can be imposed
  Updated to exclude Methamphetamine

<u>Diversion/Deferred Prosecution Alternatives</u>
  Prosecutors have statutory authority to offer diversion
    Offered Pre-charging
    Private Contractor Administers
    75% Success over life of program
    Sliding Fee Scale
    Reimbursement form provider to MCAO for administrative costs
  Statute updated pursuant to prosecutor request
    can now offer diversion with 1 prior felony conviction

<u>Drug Court</u>
  Informed by HOPE Project, close judicial supervision, frequent UAs, quick consequences

Lastly, I will list the other programs that we have for crime reduction. We have prisoner reentry programs, community partnerships, community corrections, adult probation programs, cognitive based therapies, and evidence driven programs. We have seen almost 77 percent successfully complete probation last year. Less than 22 percent were revoked and of that less

MARC LEVIN: There are a lot of things to keep in mind when comparing different states. When you look at the numbers in Arizona you have to consider that they have a higher percentage of offenders that are violent and career criminals. In Texas we have a different structure in our sentencing laws, as we have a lot more discretion, and a great deal of variation across the state. We have seventeen thousand people in Texas imprisoned for drug possession. One thing that we will hopefully get to in Q and A, is the result of this study, and whether they have a better sense of the background of people in prison. In Texas, we have a separation of the court data and the TDCJ data. We do not know how many people are first time offenders. We can only tell if they have a previous incarceration from TDCJ. I think that this data will be very valuable for policy makers in making smart decisions.

Sen. John Whitmire
Chairman, Corrections Committee, Texas State Senate

> SENATOR JOHN WHITMIRE *represents the 15th Senatorial District comprised of north Houston and parts of Harris County. He was elected to the Texas Senate in 1982 after serving 10 years in the Texas House of Representatives. With over 30 years of service in the Texas Senate, Senator Whitmire ranks first in seniority and is the "Dean of the Texas Senate." Senator Whitmire serves as Chair of the Senate Criminal Justice Committee and works to bring about needed changes to the adult and juvenile criminal justice systems. He is also a member of the Senate Administration Committee and the Senate Business and Commerce Committee. In addition, he serves as a member of the Senate Finance Committee where he is committed to finding appropriate solutions for funding the state's many agencies and programs. Originally from Hillsboro, Texas, Senator Whitmire moved to Houston where he graduated from Waltrip High School. He earned a Bachelor of Arts degree from the University of Houston and attended the Bates College of Law. He was admitted to the Texas State Bar in 1981 and is attorney of counsel to the law firm Locke Lord LLP. Senator Whitmire has two daughters and one grandson.*

First of all, we need to remember that the criminal justice system is a system. We may focus on incarceration, but we need to look at the policeman/woman on the street, the prosecutors, the probation department, parole, and the reentry program. Malfunctions on any of these levels will create problems. Getting different sectors, Shannon, to recognize that they are a part of the system has been one of our challenges throughout the years.

I would like to speak about the adult system now. First of all, I was in three prisons yesterday, a state jail, an intermediate sanction facility, and a halfway house. I would give our adult system passing grades. We shut down two prisons last session, Mineral Wells State and the Dallas State Jail, which saved ninety-eight million dollars during the interim. We closed the central unit the session before last, and saved millions of dollars without experiencing any compromise of public safety. We did not need the client space because of diversion alternative programs. I give it passing grades, but I still run into flaws. At the intermediate sanction facility, one of our reforms that ensured that instead of parole violators being re-incarcerated they were sent to this facility for up to nine months. I was there yesterday and while visiting with one of the wardens, and asked, "Once you have served your time, how do you get out?" They responded, "You do this time and then you have a halfway house opportunity." I said, "No, what door?" I wanted them to put a face on it. They said that usually they would leave a halfway house would pick you up, but if not, then they would leave out the backdoor at 6:30 in the morning. "What if you do not have money?" Being released in the streets of Houston, downtown, at 6:30 in the morning, you don't have many options. You are a parolee; you have been labeled and profiled. You probably have a mental health issue. If you do not have money, you don't have a chance. We are working on this right now. With the state jail, they have a reentry officer. She lines up housing, hopefully some food, or even job opportunities.

We still have work to do. We have work at the adult level in mental health. We still have thousands of people incarcerated, when their main problem was that they were mental health patients that could not get services. They were into drugs, or assaulted someone, and now are introduced into the criminal justice system. We are doing so much now with military courts. We have recognized the emotional problems there that will land veterans in the criminal justice system. We are also looking at prostitution. We have three hundred prostitutes in Gatesville this afternoon. Three felony convictions for prostitution will get you up to five years in prison. I am on the human trafficking interim study. The women that are were sentenced to this years ago, we are calling victims today. Help me, legislators, stakeholders. Why can we not realize that if we are calling those involved in the same situation today victims, then those before were victims as well? Why are we incarcerating them, Shannon? We need to give them an opportunity to raise their case.

Another area where we cannot be wasteful of our resources is misdemeanor arrests for two or less ounces of marijuana. Twenty-three thousand of them ended up on misdemeanor probation. I want my probation officers looking after people that we are concerned about, such as people that have assaulted someone or stole property. I do not think that the people of Texas want to spend their resources supervising twenty-three thousand people when their crime was two ounces of marijuana or less.

I was with the top brass yesterday and my staff gave me a list of all hundred and eight prisons. We are concerned about the low number of correction officers. Most are being staffed at sixty to seventy percent of needed personnel. I wanted to know what prisons were being underserved. I noticed how many prisons had only a few hundred people in them. I asked Bryan Collier, the assistant director, why they never approached legislators and tried to merge these places. Our administrators are not proactive in Texas. When we closed prisons we had to drag them along. They will give testimony, but I need administrators giving us ideas and suggestions.

The juvenile system is going to get a lot of focus. We have had some great successes there. In '07 we had five thousand people incarcerated in ten locations. We are now down to a thousand youth. Today you have to be a felon, or even have committed multiple felonies. This means that we have a very hard juvenile population. That agency leads all state agencies in workman comp claims. You may find this hard to imagine Mr. Montgomery, but on any given day seventy percent of our employees show up to work scared. There are gangs. Most youth do not get the services that they need. They do not receive the mental health, drug, and alcohol treatment that they need, or the education that they need. It is not uncommon for these facilities to be locked down for the safety of the workers and students. It is going to be hard, but we need to get away from playing politics with our clients. It is not about economics and building businesses and creating jobs in these communities, it is about public safety and sending home a better youth that was received.

Around the country I see people that want to save money and improve public safety. We are deciding the smart thing to do, not just the cheapest or the toughest. We were short of correctional officers, and the leadership wanted to build three more, when we could not run the hundred and eight that we have. We need to talk about raising the professionalization of our corrections officers, increasing the pay and raising the standards. We have come a long way, but we have farther to go.

Rep. Tan Parker

Chairman, Committee on Corrections, Texas House of Representatives

> TAN PARKER *is entering his fifth-term as a state representative representing House District 63 that includes the southwestern portion of Denton County. He has a broad executive business background in sales, marketing, management, consulting and development strategies, and is a partner in an international private equity firm. His passion has been economics and identifying free market strategies. As a legislator, Parker serves as the Chairman of the Corrections Committee*

where he continues to strive to bring improved efficiencies to the state's prison system while taking measures to enhance public safety. As Chairman, Parker oversaw the passage of more than 25 new laws regarding the state's correctional systems during the 83rd Legislative Session. Included in these reforms was the enactment of the very critical Sunset legislation necessary to overhaul, modernize and reauthorize the operations of our state's correctional systems. In an effort to be ready to get to work immediately once the legislative session starts, Chairman Parker's committee has held numerous hearings recently on such important topics as the functions of TDCJ, how to more effectively treat mental illness and substance dependency within our prison population, the appropriate role that the private sector can play in delivering corrections related services and others. Parker is a graduate of the University of Dallas and holds a Masters degree from the London School of Economics. He also serves on numerous boards from the Denton County Children's Advocacy Center to Communities in Schools of North Texas, to the University of Dallas Board of Trustees. Parker resides in Flower Mound with his wife Beth and two daughters, Lauren and Ashley.

Thank you, Marc, for having me. I want to thank you for your leadership and all that TPPF and Right on Crime does. It is a tremendous privilege to be here with my colleagues. In particular, I thank you, Senator Whitmire, for your leadership and your mentoring last session. I will really just be hitting some of the highlights, and then yielding my time for more Q and A. I think that would be most productive.

First and foremost, the interim charges were pretty comprehensive. That report will be out in the next couple of days. In the next couple of days you will see the overview of what we touched on in our review. I will tell you that I do think that the system has significantly improved. I think that we are making significant, if incremental, progress. I think that the administration is doing a good job. They are not perfect, there is lots of opportunity for improvement. But we are on the right path. One of the major hearings that I had dealt with mental health. This was one of the big discussions in the Senate and House, because frankly, our jails have become the repositories of many people dealing with mental health challenges. We need to be more intelligent with our handling of these cases. At the end of the day, Senator Whitmire is right, you have too look at the system from beginning to end.

We need to find ways to partner with the private sector in order to find employment opportunities and housing. We are not giving these people a fair shake, especially when they have mental health issues. It is very clear to me that we have to focus our time and energies on the reentry process.

Now, with regard to Right on Crime, let me make a couple of comments. I fundamentally believe that what we are seeing in the data is not by accident. It is deliberate policy that Senator Whitmire and my colleagues in the House have been pursuing over a number of years in order to get us where we are today. But there is opportunity for further improvement in this area. In reality, so many of these non-violent drug offenses are piling up and we are kicking the consequences down the road. We need to engage in this problem with counseling and psychotherapy, as opposed to incarceration. Jails are here for a reason, but that is for the violent populations that can harm people. I am also looking at innovative ways for us to be able to address some of the funding needs that we have for specific programs. My committee has been looking at social impact bonds over the interim.

If you look at some of the successful SIB programs that have been implemented here and around the world, there are very clear milestones up front for a project. Something that I find so attractive is that the state of Texas would not incur any cost for an SIB program unless it achieves the milestone targeted. In other words, we will not pay for marginal results. We will only pay for exceptional performance.

In particular we have opportunities with our juvenile population, our area of greatest need. I am very proud of the fact that we closed to prisons last session. We saved roughly a hundred million dollars. It is important that people understand that these are not Republican or Democrat issues. They are common sense issues. I think that we will continue to work in a very bipartisan manner to address challenges and to continue to be tough on crime when needed. I will cede the balance of my time for Q and A.

Q&A

MARC LEVIN: I wanted to discuss the question of truth-in-sentencing. Adam, I was wondering if you could address what you have seen in terms of public opinion on this question. Do people care more about the number of years that someone has served or what percentage of their sentence they serve?

ADAM GELB: We have done pretty extensive public opinion research on this issue. What is fascinating is that people have a strong preference for a high percent of sentence served that for a high amount of time served. One of the ways that I devised to ask this question was to ask if you would prefer someone to serve four years of a five year sentence or the same offender serve six years of a ten year sentence. The results showed in the high seventies if not the eighties that people preferred the shorter amount of time in prison.

We also have an issue with max-outs. Around the country we did a report, which showed that about 23 percent of inmates are actually serving their sentences and being released to the streets with no supervision. This is not common sense, and the research shows that it makes more sense to have a transition supervision period afterwards. In Texas, the max-out rate is about seventeen percent. Most recently we asked people about this, making a distinction between violent and non-violent offenders. We found that people definitely make a distinction between violent and non-violent offenders and how they want them to be treated. We asked people if they would rather a non-violent offender serve three years of a three-year sentence and be released, or two years followed by one year of supervision. For violent offenders we asked if they would rather serve five years of a five-year sentence or four years of a five year sentence followed by a year of supervision. The resulting percentages were in the seventies or eighties and showed that people prefer the shorter sentence, followed by a period of supervision, even for the violent offenders. The pollsters were surprised at how high the percentages were, they though it showed a pretty intensely held belief.

BILL MONTGOMERY: Regardless of what the sentence is, people want to see supervision after a sentence for a violent offender. We are looking into that reentry period of time in Arizona as well. We are identifying offenders most amenable to diversion on the front end as well as intervening on the back end.

QUESTION: Within the state or even nationally do you see any programs that are looking at true forgiveness where after a certain time a former felon is forgiven and given all his rights as a full citizen and even the possibility of his record being cleared?

BILL MONTGOMERY: Within Arizona, after a period of time and particularly if it's a first felony offense, once you've completed your sentence, whether that's from incarceration or after probation, your rights are automatically restored, with the exception of the right to possess and own a firearm. You have to petition for that after a couple of more years. Depending upon the original offense, it is usually granted. If it's two felonies or more, it's entirely discretionary with the original judge who handled it. As far as expungment of a record, there are other states around the country that are looking at some instances where people have gone a significant period of time, generally if someone goes seven years or more without having any contact with the criminal justice system, you can say they are completely rehabilitated. You'll never see them again. They're starting to look at some of those with the initial category of offenses dealing with substance abuse, drug possession, and drug use.

MARC LEVIN: Yeah, and that's excellent. In Texas, we have both non-disclosure and expunction. Non-disclosure is if you get deferred adjudication probation. One of the challenges with that is if it's a felony, you have to wait nine years typically, because it's four years of probation and then five years waiting period after that. We'd like to look at reducing some of those waiting periods during this session.

SHANNON EDMONDS: I've got a question for our two legislators. We've had a lot of data here today from a private group and from our counterpart in Arizona, TDCA, who had to pay for their own study of who's being sent to prison. We have a problem here in this state. Mr. Fabelo used to be a state employee and his office was line item vetoed in 2003 and it has not been back since. There is not a week that goes by that I don't get a question from a reporter or someone in the capital asking me for data. We just don't have it. Everybody tries to do what they can, but it's a much stripped down version. I wonder if there's been any discussion, now that we're going to have a new governor who might be more amenable to that idea of reconstituting the old criminal justice policy council so that we can have good information on which to base our future policy decisions.

JOHN WHITMIRE: I don't know where you been, but our new governor and his colleagues want less government. I don't think they're inclined to start a new agency even if it might prove to be a cost saver. Obviously I have trouble getting data and let me tell you how bad it is. TDCJ does not have any data. You walk the halls of a prison and you ask about a particular inmate, they'll send down to their office and they get a three by five card and there's pretty much where he's from, what's the nature of his crime, how many grievances he's filed, and so on. Data processing and information is very inadequate in the adult system. Fabelo is a state asset who was wrongfully removed in '03 for being candid and straightforward in finance.

Why doesn't your organization advocate? Why doesn't your organization talk about how it would enhance public safety if we knew who we were locking up and what the performance – and have some transparency and accountability. That would be a great project for you and I'll recognize you if I'm calling witnesses. I mean, that's how we would get there - with you and your credibility advocating that. It'd be probably much more effective than me doing it as everybody knows I love Fabelo. We all need data.

TAN PARKER: I concur with the Senator that we're not going to grow government. I just don't see that there's a desire to do that. I think we could be more intelligent about data though. I agree that we need to look for ways to have a greater number of public private partnerships in this area to create data. One of the issues that I see is that I'm told they're collecting data in some part of TDCJ, but it's siloed. It's an issue of connecting all of the data to where you have really a dashboard view of what's really going on. We need data that means something as opposed to data in a silo type of approach. Data is the biggest thing, as chairman of that committee that I was frustrated to have enough of and I think everybody in this room that studies the issues feels the same way. I think there are more intelligent ways to get there than growing government with a new agency. We need to be intelligent about it.

JOHN WHITMIRE: I'll be cynical for a moment. I'm not sure TDCJ wants us to have all their data.. As long as we don't have a study group, a think tank such as Fabelo's, all the information we have is what they furnish us with, which is not healthy. I agree with you, but it is reality.

ADAM GELB: Can I just say quickly, notice what this conversation's about. You have the prosecutor's association saying, we want data and the chairman of the committee saying, we want data. Not until recently would there be a committee chairman and folks and a prosecutor from Arizona coming with data to this discussion and making this conversation about data, asking questions about it. I think it's worth just noticing how far this conversation has come from one that was totally based on emotion and ideology to one that is now more and more based on research and data.

BILL MONTGOMERY: One of the reasons for that is that throwing laws out without determining whether or not they are affecting public policy is ridiculous. We asked these questions in Arizona, and we believe that our policies are oriented towards incarcerating the most violent and repetitive offenders. Before we did not know if we were doing this. This mean that we had to find out who was in prison. That is a cornerstone.

JOHN WHITMIRE: In Texas we really need to distinguish one community from another. We need to know what is going on in Bexar County versus Harris County or Dallas County. It is very frustrating to know that within the same state with the same state laws you can get completely different outcomes based on county. There are probably fifteen hundred misdemeanor confines in the Harris County jail this afternoon because they cannot afford a thousand dollars to pay bond. If they were in Dallas or Travis County they could get a PR bond and be at work today. Harris County's jails are overcrowded because they do not have a pre-release program. I would love the data, but someone needs to put some sunlight on the difference in type and degree of justice that you get depending on where you are.

QUESTION: I know Windham School District's taking a lot of kids inside. Are there programs to attach these guys to education when they get out or are there other programs looking at that? And if not, is there interest?

JOHN WHITMIRE: The answer's no, but there is interest.

TAN PARKER: I would say it is certainly of interest. In fact, I had a conversation with Clint Carpenter maybe ten days before Christmas about this very topic. We were looking at some new things that are out there that we can look at to help these individuals transition back into life. Some of these practical life skills that they don't necessarily learn getting a GED equivalent, that they need to have. It's early in the process, but we need to do more in that area.

QUESTION: My question is for Mr. Montgomery. You mentioned using cognitive behavioral therapy in reentry programs. If it works well in reentry programs, and if you could elaborate on the data, and how it works, why not move it back to when the person's still incarcerated for reentry? If you can take hardened criminals and use behavioral therapy and have a much higher success rate on reentry, why not start it sooner? That would be the common sense and inexpensive and humane thing to do.

BILL MONTGOMERY: If I had had ten more minutes, I would have covered that while I was at the podium. That's exactly what I have started advocating for. Our DOC has looked at implementing that program for close and maximum-security prisoners to deal with them when they've committed a violent offense while they're in that setting. The two that I was specifically referencing for community partners, are private partners, and the recidivism rates run ten to fifteen percent. So they've got eighty-five and ninety percent success and they're using cognitive behavioral therapies as parts of that. If anybody's interested, Dr. Stanton Samenow, *Inside the Criminal Mind*, 3rd Edition is where I got all that information. One of the recommendations is to take that program and use it for everybody when they are admitted into prison and start working it there.

We need to turn our idea of prisons upside down because right now when you go into prison, you start off in general population, which is segmented by the nature of your offense, what your reputation is and the color of your skin or the gang you're a member of. Those aren't the kind of values we want people to have to be successful when they leave and reintegrate into society. General population is close to what someone's going to be living in when they leave prison and reflects the social mores and values that are going to allow them to be successful. That kind of therapy, from the outset, I think would be very helpful.

QUESTION: This is for Senator Whitmire and Representative Parker. Given what he just said about the high success rate, do we have any bills coming up in the upcoming session in the state of Texas to fund that and to do that if the payback is so good? It sounds like a very virtuous thing to do.

JOHN WHITMIRE: I did not hear that it was being implemented yet, but let me tell you how screwed up we are. I said that our facilities get passing grades, which is a relative term. Today, regardless of how long we serve or what your offense was, those that require and offer rehabilitation are given it the last six months of the sentence. Someone can be admitted to TDCJ this afternoon, serve ten to fifteen years, and be a general population inmate. First you are sent to the fields, then you might have and opportunity to get an inside job. The average increase in education in TDCJ is one year, regardless of the time spent inside. I am concerned about the parolees and their education, but I would rather educate them while we have them. If we had the resources and the leadership in TDCJ, why would we not give the inmate rehabilitation, requiring him or her to go to classes at the front end? Inmates often try to fake it until they make it, but they eventually benefit. Would they not benefit when we first receive them? They would be better inmates. I would think that correctional officers would find it was a better environment. We have a bunch of work to do, there are waiting lists now. I cannot imagine what this does to morale. We have such a massive system. We have one and a half of Waco, Texas locked up. We have made improvements, but we have a lot to do. We spend three billion taxpayer dollars on this system; we cannot afford to waste any monies.

TAN PARKER: In summary, let me make one comment. I do think you'll see legislation that will be filed that deals with more intelligent rehabilitation type issues during this session.

BILL MONTGOMERY: In fact, out of fairness for state level legislators in Texas, I helped fund the reentry programs I was referring to out of my asset forfeiture monies at the county level. Our state doesn't provide any dollars.

QUESTION: I just wanted to know what, in the panelists' opinions, is the public safety component of low level marijuana users and why is a criminal record for low level marijuana users necessary?

JOHN WHITMIRE: Historically, the legislature has been reflecting public sentiment. Today, I think the public is in a changing mood on this and other issues. I think we just have to see after the new members are sworn in where we are. When I got to the legislature in '73, one joint was a felony. People were going to prison, and I can remember Jim Mattox and his legislation in '73, so obviously social mores change. I think you're witnessing certainly that on low-level amounts of marijuana. You know how I feel; we have to prioritize public safety. Jail cells are an asset. Prison cells are an asset. You shouldn't waste them on people you're not afraid of. Don't get after the people you're mad at. I think we're in a public discussion about how much of a danger low-level marijuana poses. Certainly, I'll let Representative Parker speak as to the aspect of medical marijuana. You know, I've visited California and Colorado, and they were different experiences.

TAN PARKER: Well, look, I think obviously what we're seeing today is based, as Senator Whitmire said, on sentiment of the public, broadly speaking, over the course of the last thirty or forty years. There is no question about that, and I do think things are changing. However, I don't like the term decriminalization. I think what you're trying to do is basically go forward with a penalty for something that's viewed as being against the rules of society. We do have to be more intelligent about the various punishments that we put in place, specifically with regard to medical marijuana. I do not think that you will ever see what has happened in California and Colorado in Texas. I never want to see Texas go that direction. Now I think there is legitimate discussion within the legislature with regard to medical marijuana for specific medical conditions. Where there is specific medical documentation and the body of knowledge, not just in Texas but also around the country, shows that medical marijuana would provide specific benefit for a particular illness, perhaps like an intractable case of childhood epilepsy, right? That's tightly written and dispensed through a pharmacy system like we do today with any other narcotic, be it oxycontin or dilaudid or any other type of narcotic that's prescribed today. Again, I think those are discussions that the legislature will probably start to have here in the 84th. I think that sentiment broadly is changing on a number of those issues.

21st Century Juvenile Justice: A Texas-Sized Problem
SEN. JOSE RODRIGUEZ | REP. JAMES WHITE | CHELSEA BUCHHOLTZ | TONY FABELO
MODERATOR: **DEREK COHEN**

Texas has made dramatic progress over the last several years in reducing juvenile incarceration and, most importantly, cutting juvenile crime. Come hear how Texas is coping with the difficulties – and capitalizing on the opportunities – unique to juvenile justice, and learn about ideas for next session that break the cycle of delinquency and put more troubled Texas kids on the right track.

This event took place at Texas Public Policy Foundation's 2015 Policy Orientation.

Derek Cohen
Senior Policy Analyst, Center for Effective Justice, Texas Public Policy Foundation
Senior Policy Analyst, Right on Crime

DEREK M. COHEN *is a policy analyst in the Center for Effective Justice at the Texas Public Policy Foundation and the Right on Crime campaign. Cohen graduated with a B.S. in Criminal Justice from Bowling Green State University and an M.S. in Criminal Justice from the University of Cincinnati, where he is currently completing his Ph.D. dissertation on the long-term costs and outcomes associated with correctional programming. His academic work can be found in Policing: An International Journal of Police Strategies & Management and the forthcoming Encyclopedia of Theoretical Criminology and The Oxford Handbook on Police and Policing, and has scholarly articles currently under review. He has presented several papers to the American Society of Criminology, the Academy of Criminal Justice Sciences, and the American Evaluation Association on the implementation and outcomes of various criminal justice policy issues. Prior to joining the Foundation, Cohen was a research associate with University of Cincinnati's Institute of Crime Science. He also taught classes in statistics, research methods, criminal procedure, and corrections.*

On behalf of the Texas Public Policy Foundation, I'd like to welcome you to our panel, "21st Century Juvenile Justice: A Texas-Sized Problem." My name is Derek Cohen and I'm a policy analyst in the Center for Effective Justice and with our Right On Crime campaign. Now the subtitle for this panel, a Texas-Sized Problem, is deliberate. The vast expanse of Texas makes organizing and administering a centralized juvenile justice system near impossible. This geographic and jurisdictional spread basically precludes any economy of scale that is enjoyed in a less substantial state. As a result of this, it costs Texans $367 per child per day to house them in a state facility. Contrast this with $31.56 to house them on post-release supervision. Add this to federal mandates and jurisprudence and it becomes a costly proposition indeed.

Still, Texas has a lot to be proud of in the area of juvenile justice. The juvenile justice apparatus has actually been able to overcome a lot of the issues that has plagued it in the past through quality oversight and leadership. Each year, fewer and fewer children are sent to state facilities here in Texas. That is in no small part due to some of the representation we have on this panel here. A research report by the Juvenile Law Center has ranked Texas as fourth in the nation for potential expunctions and confidentiality of juvenile records, thereby preventing collateral consequences farther down the line for juvenile deviants. TJJD specifically, in the medley of the job functions of the Texas Youth Commission and the Texas Juvenile Probation Authority has managed to keep nominal spending on par with 2001 levels, which actually led to a real savings of twenty-two million dollars between FY 2012 and FY 2014 alone. Most importantly, this has not come at any cost to public safety.

All of this is not to say that we here in Texas and in the Juvenile Justice Department should be resting on our laurels. There are still many things that need to be addressed. Texas is one of the few states that uses the criminal justice system to address truancy issues. Status offenders could still end up in jail should they be found in violation of a juvenile court order and that court order is for a crime that would not be so should the individual be an adult. Texas has by far and away the most onerous training requirements for our correctional officers at three hundred hours. This requirement is so high that if we were to eliminate two and a half weeks worth of the curriculum, we would still be tied for first place. This state has also dragged its feet in closing a juvenile justice facility by still keeping a skeleton crew that is hemorrhaging money by the day. Texas has accomplished a great deal and still has a lot left to accomplish.

This is actually what brings us here today. The question, put most simply, is what can we do to best provide public safety, the most bang for the taxpayer dollar, and the best justice for the youth that are involved in the juvenile justice system? As you can see, we've assembled quite the august panel here of stakeholders and lawmakers to discuss this issue. And after the presentation is concluded, we will have an opportunity for questions and answers.

Dr. Tony Fabelo
Director of Research, Council of State Governments Justice Center

> TONY FABELO *is in charge of designing, developing, and implementing the research agenda for the Justice Center. He also provides technical assistance to state and local governments to help increase public safety and make more efficient use of state and local taxpayer dollars. Before joining the CSG Justice Center, he was a Senior Research Associate with the JFA Institute. Between 1984 and 2003, he worked with the Texas Criminal Justice Policy Council, and was appointed by Governor Ann Richards to head this state research and evaluation agency in 1991. He continued to serve as Director under Governor George W. Bush and Governor Rick Perry. During Dr. Fabelo's tenure on the Council, he advised five governors from both sides of the aisle. He has also assisted every legislature since 1985 in developing criminal justice policies, including crafting the major justice reinvestment initiative adopted by the Texas legislature in 2007. The U.S. Attorney General appointed him to the Office of Justice Programs Science Advisory Panel in 2010. In 2012, Dr. Fabelo was selected to serve in the National Academy of Sciences panel on the Cause and Consequences on High Incarceration Rates, which will issue a national report in 2014 on this subject. He received his B.A. in Political Science from Loyola University, and his M.A. and Ph.D. from the University of Texas at Austin.*

We are about to release a study that looks at the whole juvenile justice system. I cannot tell you the findings as yet, but might be able to give you an idea of what questions we are addressing. I also want to make some general observations, looking back at the seventeen legislative sessions I have had, and the eighteenth is coming up.

In this study we tracked three hundred thousand juveniles in Texas starting in 2006 until 2012. We focused on a group of TYC-eligible kids, fifty-five thousand of them and looked at three questions. The first was, had the population of TYC facilities impacted public safety? As you know, the commitments to TYC declined from 2,7000 in 2006 to 800 last year. The population decline from 4,700 to about 1,000 last year. The question is, has this decline impacted recidivism? We will be able to answer that, looking at very complex motive, varying analysis model of all the records of these kids that we have tracked. The second question that we are looking at is whether the increase in probation funding has positively impacted recidivism outcomes. The probation system has seen a ninety-eight percent increase in per capita expenditure between 2005 to 2012. We are spending more to put children on probation than what we spend educating a child in Texas, about 8,569 per year. That was about 4,337 dollars in 2005-2005 and it begs the question, what has been the impact on recidivism? We will have an answer to that. The third question is, what have we learned after all of this? We looked at Travis County, Harris County, El Paso, and Dallas, at each of their systems. We wanted to know what lessons we could learn and how we could apply that to a model that would improve the system. That report will be release on January 29 in the Supreme Court chambers at 10 o'clock.

Florida, a growing state with a high young, Hispanic population, in 2006 saw a thirty-five percent decrease in arrests. In California there was a forty-eight percent decrease in arrests. However, Texas saw a thirty-one percent increase in arrests. In other states you do not see that. I do not have a good answer for that. I think that kids are spending more time inside on the Internet. Some techniques have improved in the system, such as supervision. We have risk-needs assessments that are routinely used, even if not well. There is a better use of electronic records and more interaction with the mental health and social services system. Probation officers are better trained than they have ever been.

Three years after release from TYC, seventy-seven percent of juveniles are rearrested. Almost forty-four percent are re-incarcerated. This usually happens in the adult system because juveniles are originally incarcerated as fifteen or sixteen year olds, they serve a few years in the TYC population and become adults there. Then when they are re-incarcerated, they go in as adults. Recidivism is high in the community population as well, more or less at fifty-three percent after three years. I am going to suggest that funding is not the issue. The probation system received thirteen thousand fewer referrals to the system than it received in 1986. It is a smaller system in great part because of the decline in arrests. Yet, the probation system budget, the state budget, not counting the local budget, is 485 percent larger than it was in 1986, adjusting for inflation. It is not an issue of money, it is an issue of how you are targeting programs.

Commission reports have repeatedly said that the agency should have an ongoing study of the most effective programs for rehabilitation of juveniles and place it as a top priority, but over and over again the agency has not done that. How many times do you need to ask them to target the state funding to maximize the impact on recidivism and accountability?

A third observation is that the youth incarceration model needs to be revisited. Issues such as the type of facilities, the dorm configuration, the type of population, high staff turnover rate, these all need to be addressed. There is a lot of money going into this system and there are very legitimate questions that we need to ask.

Hopefully this study will set the tone for a methodical look at outcomes and co-relationships with local systems.

Chelsea Buchholtz
General Counsel, Texas Juvenile Justice Department

CHELSEA BUCHHOLTZ *joined TJJD in August of 2012 as deputy general counsel and became general counsel in April of 2014. She is a former Texas Governor's appointee of the Juvenile Justice Services and Facilities Transition Team, which coordinated and oversaw the transition of services and facilities during the formation of TJJD. She previously worked as a policy advisor for the Office of the Governor Budget, Planning, and Policy Division, handling matters pertaining to criminal and juvenile justice, public safety, and military and veterans' affairs. She is a former assistant general counsel for the Office of the Governor, a former briefing attorney of the Texas Court of Appeals Fourth District, and is a member of the State Bar of Texas. Chelsea received a bachelor's degree from Abilene Christian University and a law degree from Pepperdine University School of Law.*

I want to make a few comments about the fairly new agency, the Texas Juvenile Justice Department. It was created in December of 2011 in the midst of what were years of reform. In some ways the merge of TYC and TJJD still continues. Most of the continued merging is related to infrastructure, a natural distinction. On one side we provide funding to counties that keep kids close to home, which is being done on higher levels than ever before. As D. Fabelo mentioned, we had less than eight hundred commitments to the state side of things last year because counties are keeping more kids. We provide regulatory oversights to counties and also technical assistance when necessary. Each juvenile county probation department is governed by a local board, they are not our employees, simply our partnership. Dr. Fabelo mentioned that there are fewer kids in the entire system today. In 2009 there were 97,000 children who entered the juvenile justice system or referred to a county juvenile probation department. Last year we only had 63,000.

The other side of our shop are the state facilities, and there as well we have a declining population. In 2007 we had more than four thousand children in state facilities. Today we have just over thirteen hundred on any given day. This includes children in our five operating high restriction facilities, the eight halfway houses, as well as contract placement. On the back end they are often placed on parole, and we have parole offices all over the state. Part of the reason for the declining population is a national trend, as well as the fact that we only take children with felonies now. Additionally the legislature has funded commitment diversion programs to keep children from penetrating the system further than they should.

Dr. Fabelo's report will be published at the end of the month and we anticipate that it will reveal a continued need for improvement of youth outcomes, system wide. Our research has shown that children need to stay close to home, in small facilities with the least restrictive environment, receiving services based on their specific needs. We have convened a work group that is meeting today with our county partners to address recidivism and keeping kids closer to home. Additionally, the focus needs to be on duplicating effective programming at the county level.

Dr. Fabelo mentioned his need for performance based-funding. Obviously we have made very slow progress on that, but this report provides perfect opportunity for that to come back to the forefront. The majority of our performance monitoring today is based on the terms of our contract with counties. Have stuck to allowable expenditures? Are their budgets accurate and reasonably based on the purpose for funding? We monitor performance in those areas and provide technical assistance to get counties back on track. If necessary we have structures in place to withhold or request refunded money. This is an area that we need to shore up. TJJD provides this to counties in a very flexible way that is intended to maintain local control and autonomy. We have been providing training to counties on how to develop programs designed to control specific outcomes, and then evaluating the programs. We still need to tie funding to that performance. We expect that to be part of this coming legislative session. However, even today, we receive refunds from counties that cannot spend the money that we give them. We should be reallocating those funds based on performance. To do so, we need a research team to measure the data that we collect.

The report refocuses our conversation back to youth outcomes, the mission of our agency. It is a perfect time for this because we have a new executive director. David Riley came to us from Bexar County, where he was for seventeen years. He is a social worker at heart; he does not give up on children. He wants to ensure that each child is given the best care that we can provide. He has said that we need to look at our current system, our facilities, our funding levels, training requirements, our system as driven through policies developed by the legislature historically over time.

The world changes, however. Policies shift, focuses change, and we expect to take direction from the legislature on whether or not the current system continues to function in the new landscape. Currently we have inadequate staffing levels. Mr. Riley was surprised to learn that we have unmanned pickets at some locations. We have correctional officers in classrooms. In some instances we have officers who watch children, but they do not have backup when something goes wrong. This may be unheard of in county facilities, but it is a reality in state facilities. Additionally, we have a high turnover. Thirty-eight percent of our turnover is our correctional staff. About half o four newly hired correctional staff leave within the first year. We train people as fast as they leave. We asked our ombudsman to focus on each facility to learn why this was happening. There were a lot of takeaways from that, one of which was that we are not training our staff to succeed. Some of these things we can address now, but some require help from the legislature. This may sound counter-intuitive, but we need to lessen the three hundred hour requirement, in order to have more resources for training in the long-term. We also need to teach our staff to be strong leaders.

We also have what I call the contagion factor. Today children with high risks are tending to bring along those that are lower risk. We spend a lot of time addressing ways to remedy these challenges. The answers are not simple, but there is some simplicity in attaining adequate staffing and training. Focusing there we can improve outcomes. It is not all about money. There are some things that we can do today. As I said earlier, if the legislature continues the decrease in the population then the current model cannot be sustained. We stand ready and willing to aid the legislature in finding a model conducive to the policy and climate in Texas today.

Sen. Jose Rodriguez
Texas State Senate

SENATOR JOSÉ RODRÍGUEZ *represents Texas Senate District 29, which includes the counties of El Paso, Hudspeth, Culberson, Jeff Davis, and Presidio. He represents both urban and rural constituencies, and more than 350 miles of the Texas-Mexico border. Prior to his election to the Texas Senate in 2010, he served as the El Paso County Attorney for 17 years, where he established an unequaled record of enhancing legal services to protect vulnerable citizens and prevent crime with a focus on rehabilitation for juveniles and drug offenders. In the 83rd Legislature, Senator Rodríguez passed fifty bills and two concurrent resolutions into law. For his efforts on civil and criminal justice issues, he was named "Legislator of the Year" by the Family Law Section of the State Bar of Texas and the "Best of the Senate" by the Combined Law Enforcement Associations of Texas. Senator Rodríguez currently serves as the Chairman of the Senate Hispanic Caucus, the Vice Chairman of the Senate Jurisprudence Committee, and as a member of the Senate Committees on Criminal Justice, Government Organization, and Veterans Affairs & Military Installations.*

I was elected in 1993. 1995 was when we had all of that "tough on crime" approaches coming in. I'm glad that we got away from that, thanks to the Texas Public Policy Foundation with their Smart on Crime program, which I support for the most part. I'd like to offer you my perspective not only as a legislator but also as a county attorney that prosecuted crime for almost twenty years. I felt strongly about those issues and subsequent to '95 I had about three or four juveniles tried ad adults. I simply do not believe in that system because of the reports coming out of Florida and other places showing that this was barely having an impact on recidivism and turning out juveniles with more criminal potential.

I agreed that we needed to hold juveniles accountable, but that we ought to be focusing on rehabilitation, diversion, and intervention. We created a teen court program in El Paso County. We needed that approach in order to focus on rehabilitating juveniles, in giving them an alternative to incarceration. I have similar perspectives as a legislator. From a policy perspective, in both the juvenile and adult systems, we need to hold them accountable and send a message, but we need to do it in a way that makes sense in the long term for society as a whole, factoring in the state's limited resources. This is especially true for teenagers that have made a mistake. Today these children are limited by having a criminal record. This limits where they are going to go to college, what kind of job they can get, whether they will live productive lives. All of these factors make it more likely that they will be marginalized by society and are more likely to commit future crimes.

From a budget perspective, handling juveniles the smart way will have a significant impact on our state. Spending on criminal justice issues absorbs about six percent of the state's budget every year. We spend about 5.1 billion incarcerating adult offenders. What is notable about this dollar amount is that nearly all of it, almost five billion, comes from the general fund, or in other words, our state funds. Particularly relevant to our discussion today, is that the last legislative session allocated 645.7 million dollars for juvenile services, and about ninety percent of that came from general revenue.

Looking at these dollar figures, it is incumbent on legislators to find ways to reduce the billions of dollars that we spend every year to incarcerate adults and juvenile offenders. This brings me back to our policy, by making significant changes we can reduce the burden placed on the system. We need to reform our current system to make sure that once sentences are served offenders, particularly juvenile offenders can finish their education and find employment.

During this session we expect several legislative efforts. I will not talk about everything that we are going to address. There are about five areas that will be at the top of the agenda. One is raising the age. Right now juveniles range from ten to sixteen years of age. Should we raise the age to seventeen? There have been a lot of studies and court decisions that speak about the neurological development of children, differentiating it from adults. It is shown that they are not as likely to consider the consequences of their actions as adults. Added to this is a susceptibility to environmental pressures and impulsive or risky behavior. The Miller decision talks about this extensively. Raising the age would ensure that seventeen year olds receive rehabilitative treatment in age appropriate settings rather than automatically going into the adult system where thy are often exposed to more harmful mental and physical conditions. There are definitely cost savings at the local level.

Another legislative effort is sentencing reform. Senate Bill 2, last session, eliminated life without parole for seventeen year olds. I was the only senator that voted against it. I voted against it because in Texas what will happen is that you will end up being sentenced to forty years before parole is eligible. My problem with that is that the US Sentencing Commission defines a life sentence as 470 months, just over thirty-nine years. Based on average life expectancy in prison, this is still life without parole. In the Miller case the court struck down the mandatory sentences for life without the possibility of parole for capital crimes committed by children under the age of eighteen. This was determined to be a violation of the 8th amendment. Tellingly, in the decision, the court said that judges and juries should be able to impose iindividualized sentences based on unique characteristics of the juvenile. These characteristics are things such as age, family, home environment, the circumstances of the homicide, and familial and peer pressure. I believe that this is a more rational way of approaching these cases. I also think that we have opened ourselves to more litigation by not allowing judges or juries to make an assessment on these factors.

I also wanted to cover the failure to attend school. I serve on the Jurisprudence Committee, and we will be looking at decriminalizing truancy. We are one of only two to six states in the country that criminalize truancy. We have more cases under our criminal truancy system than all other states combined. We need to do something about this. That is one of our recommendations in the Jurisprudence Committee. Another issue is the way that we handle juvenile records. Representative White and I passed legislation during the last session that created an advisory committee to examine the fingerprinting practices of juveniles. This committee comprised of several stakeholders, including TJJD. Additionally the committee members recommended that we create another advisory committee to examine best practices around the dissemination and confidentiality of juvenile records.

Finally, status offenses will also be discussed. Running away, breaking curfew, consuming and possessing alcohol, these are status offenses, and they are really clouding up our courts. We need to focus more on providing community services, such as tutoring. These are less expensive and more effective. Overall juveniles end up in our system either because of family or systemic issues. Locking them up places pressures on limited state and local resources, but does little to rehabilitate them. We should instead focus on investing on prevention, diversion, and providing services in the community setting. I look forward to working with the Foundation as well as the agency folks and my fellow legislators to bring about some of these reforms.

Rep. James White
Texas House of Representatives

REPRESENTATIVE JAMES WHITE *is a native Texan and grew up in Houston, where he attended public schools. He graduated with honors from Prairie View A&M University in 1986 with a degree in political science and military science. The United States Congress subsequently commissioned James as an officer of Infantry in the U.S. Army, where he served his country in assignments throughout the world, most notably from 1987-90 in the Berlin Brigade during the demise of the Soviet Union. After separating from the Army with an Honorable Discharge in 1992, James began a career as a public school educator in the Houston area. He completed doctoral studies in political science at the University of Houston and has taught the social sciences on the middle school, high school, and undergraduate collegiate levels. James has also coached high school football and basketball and officiated youth sports in his spare time. Elected to the Texas House of Representatives in 2010, James is a strong advocate for the residents of District 19 and committed to ensuring the people of Hardin, Jasper, Newton, Polk, and Tyler counties are well represented in their state legislature. James is a passionate and effective advocate for the fundamental values of strong families, constitutional government, lower taxes, and economic prosperity. He puts those values into practice as a member of the Republican Caucus, Tea Party Caucus, Legislative Black Caucus, Rural Caucus, Manufacturing Caucus, Energy Caucus, and the Texas Conservative Coalition. He currently serves on the Joint Committee on Human Trafficking, the Agriculture and Livestock Committee and is the Vice Chairman of the Corrections Committee.*

The next legislative session should be interesting. Where I started in 2011, we had this big merger. There are a lot of different theories on what motivations there were there. From my perspective as a freshman it was a budget scenario. We wanted to do right by the kids, but it was the budget crisis that instigated the process. That said, I am very proud of the stakeholders and the people at TJJD.

Listening to our researchers, the high recidivism rate caught my attention, especially for juveniles involved in our facilities. We need to wonder what the rationale is behind that. One hypothesis is that as the population decreased, we were receiving tougher kids. It is possible that whatever programs that we use are not suited for that population. We need to understand that the counties are sending the tougher kids. However, in the counties recidivism is still high. This is something that we need to look into.

We need to challenge the conventional wisdom. I filed several truancy decriminalization bills and received a few calls from justices of the peace. I had a talk with an assistant principal. I was a schoolteacher before I was elected, and if I had continuously sent children to the office, I would not have a job. That is not an effective disciplinary technique. Kids are removed from the classroom. However, some local officials believe that rounding challenging kids up and putting them in jail is an effective tool to keep people in school. Mirabeu B. Lamar, the father of Texas public education, said that the whole idea of having a public education system is to teach people their rights and responsibilities as free citizens in a republic. We need to come up with some new techniques. I spoke with a principal from my district today, who believes that without this tool he will not be able to get people in school. However, he says that he makes sure that these kids are only in jail over the weekend, and are not being removed from the classroom. We need to keep challenging the conventional wisdom.

Q&A

DEREK COHEN: Senator Rodriguez, you mentioned raising the age. I would like to ask every member what their opinion is on this from their particular vantage point.

TONY FABELO: I do not have a particular opinion. If we change the age, someone needs to a very good analysis of what this will do to the numbers in the system. It will have fiscal and local implications. Situations are very individualized and it will depend on the circumstances.

CHELSEA BUCHHOLTZ: TJJD will do exactly what the legislature tells us to do. There are arguments for and against raising the age. If it does change, we will need to be given time to plan and organize.

SEN. RODRIGUEZ: I would say that we should raise the age to seventeen. Dr. Fabelo is right, there are consequences to it. There are fiscal consequences and consequences regarding the way that the agency is run. As it is, the Miller decision governs children under eighteen. In my opinion, you can have fourteen year olds that are cold-blooded killers, just the same as cold-blooded seventeen year olds. The issue is that they are still children. Treating them as adults will not allow them to receive the services that will rehabilitate them. That is my reasoning for raising the age.

REP. JAMES WHITE: I am open on the question. I do not think that society right now wants to hold people accountable. At seventeen I was a young soldier working with all of the implements of violence in order to protect the freedom of this country. I had responsibility. There are a lot of variables, and the move needs to make sense. Sending a fourteen or fifteen year old to jail because they missed a few days of school does not make sense. However, a seventeen year old that commits a mass killing? They need adult intervention. I will just continue to listen to the debate, and try to get stakeholders around the table to discuss this.

SEN. RODRIGUEZ: I want to add that there are several states already that treat seventeen year olds as juveniles. The sky has not fallen there, but it also means that treatment is just an matter of geography, which does not make any sense.

CHELSEA BUCHHOLTZ: Forty states have a maximum age of seventeen, and eight have maximum age of sixteen.

QUESTION: I am a state representative from Illinois. Illinois has raised the age. As a police officer I initially hated it, but now law enforcement has gotten behind the change. It passed with strong bipartisan support. The Illinois Juvenile Justice Commission actually put forth the study that resulted in the legislation. As someone who was formerly in law enforcement, specializing in juvenile matters, I think that it worked out well. Some of the changes are just window dressing in my opinion, but I would love to know what Texas is doing. I think that the time is right, and that people across the nation are yearning for it. I would love to glean information. I want to take back what you guys are doing, because the nation looks at Texas.

SEN. RODRIGUEZ: I think you received the handout that the Texas Public Policy Foundation has on a lot of the items. That encapsulates what we are going to be doing. Some of those initiatives may not succeed. There are some that I wanted more information on myself. I come from a different spectrum of the political arena. I think that you will get a sense of what it is that we are going to be working on and why.

REP. WHITE: On a practical note, have a lot of people at the table, and lean on your local government officials. I think that in Texas our counties tend to be more independent. Even though they are political subdivisions of the state, they have a level of independence. Whatever we do in the legislature, local levels will have to implement, so consult them.

Rethinking Mental Health: Are We Throwing the Right Life Lines to People with Mental Illness?

LEON EVANS | COLLEEN HORTON | ANDREW KELLER
MODERATOR: **KATE MURPHY**

Mental Health is on many legislators' minds as we move into this coming legislative session. Panelists will critically discuss the implications of mental health practices and policies that mental healthcare advocates are promoting. In light of the Sunset Commission's recommendations for the Department of State Health Services, legislators must consider whether the mental health services available in Texas are actually providing the right kind of help. This panel will discuss the future of mental healthcare and the most prudent ways to move toward a more efficient, effective system of care.

This event took place at Texas Public Policy Foundation's 2015 Policy Orientation.

Kate Murphy
Mental Health Fellow, Texas Public Policy Foundation

KATE E. MURPHY *is the Mental Health Policy Fellow contributing to the centers for Effective Justice and Health Care at the Texas Public Policy Foundation. Kate interned for Justice Johnson at the Texas Supreme Court. She was also a Judge K.K. Legett Fellow. As part of the program Kate interned at the Washington Legal Foundation where she drafted arguments that were included in amicus briefs submitted to the U.S. Supreme Court. Before joining the Foundation, Kate worked as an attorney in Houston. Her practice focused primarily on oil and gas law and condemnation proceedings. Kate graduated magna cum laude from Austin College with a B.A. in Economics and Political Science. During her time at Austin College Kate collaboratively wrote and published policy analysis inDismantling Terrorism: Developing Actionable Solutions for Today's Plague of Violence for the 50th Annual U.S. Air Force Academy Academic Assembly and helped plan and facilitate the Economic Scholars Program with the Federal Reserve Bank of Dallas as part of the Peer Review Board. She earned her law degree from Texas Tech University School of Law where she was inducted into the National Order of Barristers for her achievements in oral advocacy and received awards for her accomplishments in constitutional law and property law.*

I'd like to welcome you to our panel on rethinking mental health care in Texas. My name is Kate Murphy, I'm going to be the moderator today. I am the mental health policy fellow at TPPF. This is relatively new territory for the Texas Public Policy Foundation and we are excited to be engaging in the conversation surrounding mental health care issues in Texas. Since I've started working at TPPF, I think one of the most profound statements that I've heard related to mental health was from Pat Deegan. She said, help isn't help if it is not helpful. Which is pretty simple, but very true. That's what we're going to be talking about here today, the types of help that would be helpful. We're going to be talking about practices, systems, and actions.

There was a cartoon that Scott Chambers drew back in 2000 called

Tested and Proven Methods of Drowning In Help. In this cartoon, there was a man drowning in the ocean, crying out, "Help!" He looks up and he sees a wheelchair fall down from the sky, and it hits him on the head and then sinks to the bottom of the ocean, along with him. I think this really reflects some of the approaches we've had to practices related to mental health care in Texas. A lot of the practices that we're seeing are not necessarily helpful. Our panelists today are going to discuss some of the best practices, that are actually going to serve people with mental illness in Texas. In the second cartoon in Scott Chambers' series, we see another man drowning in the ocean, crying out, "Help! Help!" All of a sudden, he looks up and he sees money raining down. He looks very happy, because, of course, money it fixes everything, but then the money hits the water and floats on top while the man continues to drown. I think this gets at some of the systemic problems we have with mental health care in Texas.

We're going to be talking about some of the systematic changes that Texas needs besides just throwing more money. Money is not the end-all, be-all of mental health care in Texas. It is not the only thing that needs changing. We have seen throughout the Sunset Commission's review of the Health and Human Services Commission and the Department of State Health Services what sort of unhelpful "help" we truly have in Texas. Finally, we're going to talk about actions, which bring me to Scott Chambers' third cartoon. You see the man again, drowning, calling out for help, and a big book entitled *Report On Drowning* falls from the sky and floats on the water while he continues to drown. This is one that resonates pretty strongly with people like myself. At a think tank, we write a lot of reports, but at TPPF, we like to think of ourselves as a 'do tank', not just a think tank. We're going to be discussing some of the actions that we can take to move Texas into the future of mental health care that we want to see, and that would make Texas really a model for the rest of the country.

Leon Evans
The Center for Health Care Services
President, Bexar County Mental Health and Substance Abuse Authority

> For the past thirty-eight years, LEON EVANS has worked tirelessly to improve the lives of people with mental illness. As President and Chief Executive Officer at The Center for Health Care Services, Evans has developed an innovative and highly integrated system of care for people in the San Antonio community who struggle with mental health disorders. Utilizing strong community partnerships and diverse funding sources, Leon's programs have created an effective public safety net that keep people with mental illness out of emergency rooms, jails and prisons and link them to treatment programs that help them lead independent, productive lives. As President/CEO, Evans has developed a number of nationally recognized initiatives including the Bexar County Jail Diversion Program; the 24/7 Crisis Care Center; Crisis Intervention Training for public safety officers; and The Restoration Center, an integrated clinic providing psychiatric care, substance abuse services, transitional housing and general health care services for the homeless population. Each year, these programs save thousands of lives and result in millions of dollars of cost savings for the community. Under Evans' leadership, The Center for Health Care Services has received many awards, including The Center for Medicaid and Medicare (CMS) Innovation Award for the integration of health care within behavioral health services, the American Psychiatric Association's Gold Award for Community Program Innovation and the National Council for Community Behavioral Healthcare's Service Excellence Award.

Twenty-five percent of everybody on this earth has a diagnosable mental illness. Most of us never get diagnosed, even though we may be drinking more than we should, we may be overusing prescription drugs, we may be having family problems, we may have problems with our kids, or at work. The serious concern is that people with severe mental illness in Texas die twenty-nine years sooner than the general population. There are many reasons for this, self-medication, lack of primary care, and high smoking and illegal substance use among the population. Then, when these people do die, they are million dollar patients, because they are dying of congestive heart failure and liver disease.

Malcolm Gladwell wrote an article for *The New Yorker* where he describes it as the Million Dollar Murray. These are the chronically and persistently homeless. If you research the cost to taxpayers for the homeless, you will get all kinds of reports. I did it three or four years ago, and the cheapest report I saw estimated that it costs about thirty thousand dollars a year to taxpayers for each individual. They have lots of contact with law enforcement; they are in and out of jail, and in and out of emergency rooms, and they cycle over and over and over again. They're kids may be taken away, and when they turn eighteen or nineteen they get out of foster care and go on the streets. Then the cycle continues.

Twenty-five to thirty percent of people in jail have diagnosable mental illnesses, and most go untreated. Can you see how the problem here is really harming the public safety net and costing taxpayers dollars? The World Health Organization and the National Institute On Health have done studies of what they call disease burden, and three of those top diseases that cost society the most money in lost productivity and actual health care costs are mental illnesses. If substance abuse was added, it would be even more prominent.

In Bexar County we have very little capita, so little that we actually were punished because we refused to have a waiting list. We still have a lot of national recognition. We were awarded the American Psychiatric Association Gold Award. We've had six or seven countries and almost every state come to visit. In fact, I was in Baton Rouge last week cause they want to implement our model. Just this past year Wyandotte County and then Johnson County, Kansas developed a program similar to our restoration center as well as Polk County, Des Moines, Iowa. When they come, they see the programs we've been able to knit together. There is a lot of local investment, this is not all state dollars. But there's just not enough dollars at the federal, state, and local level to handle this problem.

So one of the things people are always excited about when they visit us is we found a way to integrate those local, state, and federal dollars and try to drive out the waste and duplication. But funders all want us to meet their reports. Every funder has a different set of outcomes, and wants to account for their money in a different way. Sometimes we kind of violate some of those trusts. We do a lot of things at the public level and policy level and funding level that don't drive outcomes. We value units of service, we value volume, but do we really value outcomes? In fact when we budgeted this last go-around I told the people that I work with that money is power. Don't bring me a budget that doesn't show three things. I want you to show me how these dollars are going to improve patient experience, how people are going to get better outcomes and how we can drive down costs. I want to know how we can be more efficient in the way we do business. Steve Forbes mentioned this, "If the only tool you have is a hammer, everything looks like a nail." We don't need everybody to see a doctor or psychologist or psychiatrist. In fact, in some of our most important programs, we use peers, people in recovery.

I could kind of go on and on, but I'll give you a quick example. We have a path program, and we have professionals who go out, under the bridges to the homeless and we try to endear ourselves to people who are mentally ill and get them in and get them into treatment. We unfortunately have a fairly high no-show rate, even though we connect with people. Eventually we hired a peer, a guy who used to be homeless and addicted and mentally ill, and who is doing really well. Well, he is able to talk to those folks because he used to be mentally ill and homeless and addicted himself. He says, "I was in the same shipwreck as you, except I got off. Don't you want to come and let me help you get off?" Then our no-show rate just plummeted. Hiring peers isn't as expensive, but they really affect people's lives, and there is a lot of motivational engagement. These are ways that we can drive better behavior, better outcomes, and that don't cost a lot of money. When people come to visit, we've got all these programs, and things they always say is how did you get everybody to work together? So we have these community collaboratives. We have one for adults. It's called the medic records round table. And we have one for children. And the one for adults is actually chaired by an emergency room physician. And hospital emergency rooms are just packed with the mentally ill. You know, they get bedded, you know, in fact San Diego Scripps Center did a study on the high utilizers in San Diego several years ago.

The Scripps Center is a famous research center in San Diego. They recently looked at the high utilizers in San Diego, and found that they were costing the country about two hundred thousand dollars a year. Unexpectedly, most of those costs were not in jails or emergency rooms, they were from hospitals. The emergency rooms are very small, and so many of these individuals are bedded in the hospitals. Then, once they are a patient, tests are done that show diseases, such as congestive heart failure and liver disease. Then they are required to provide treatment. Now law enforcement has been brought to the table, consumers and families have been brought to the table; we have brought the medical community, as well as the judiciary. We are not a bureaucratic entity. I give control of my local and state dollars to have the community help me figure out how to solve these problems.

We collected a lot of data on costs and outcomes. Every one gets to see it, and some people say that that is a problem, so we change our practices, what we do, to see what actually works. If not, we try something else. When we started our jail diversion program the biggest problem was not mental illness, it was alcohol and drugs. However, Texas did not fund treatment for alcohol and drug problems. Eventually we decided to find a way to sober and detox these people. We started a homeless program called

Haven for Hope. It was the vision of Bill Greehey, the past president and CEO for Valero, as well as being the most generous, kind person that I have ever met. He saw a TV show about the homeless and got involved. The mayor was smart enough to put him in front of a task force, and now we have this Haven for Hope campus. It is about a hundred and seven million dollar campus, but the homeless count in downtown is seventy percent.

Remember, I told you earlier the chronically and persistently homeless are people with mental illness and substance abuse. The county judge calls me up and says, "Leon, don't we do some things for the homeless?" I said, "Well, yes, Judge Wolff." He knew Mr. Greehey was going to hit him up for some operational money. I met with Bill Greehey in his office. He was talking about the fact that he wasn't going to give handouts to people, instead he wanted to give them a hand up. If you actually go to Haven of Hope main campus, you have to sign a transformational pledge that says you'll be alcohol and drug free and that you will work eight hours a day. I know some single moms who are put through nursing school and other people going through welding school and stuff. It is not like most shelters, it is not there so that you can get a place to sleep and a warm meal, and then you get kicked out on the street the next morning. If we became jobless one day, we could get a job the next, but these people are sick and impaired. They walk right out the door, they start panhandling, drinking and doing drugs. Sometimes we are reinforcing or enabling them to stay sick and ill, but that is not Greehey. He did not give his money away merely to feel good. He gave his money away to help people.

We also have a central health care that is CMS, we have health care innovation grants, recently. We got one of those, we're bringing primary care. And when I was visiting with Mr. Greehey, I basically told him his plan wouldn't work because there was no capacity. And so I said, your plan won't work because there's no capacity to treat the, you know, the people that really cost society the most money. And I could tell he was interested and he helped champion us getting some money from the legislature to renovate what's called the Restoration Center now for everybody – and one year's treatment. Senator Ogden didn't want the state to have to pay for that ongoing, so the deal was is that we'd keep data. If we could prove up to the local community that this was saving them money and they would, you know, invest then we could keep it going.

I had to tell Mr. Greehey that his plan would not work because there was no capacity. In 2000 the Bexar County jail was being cited by the Health and Standards Commission for overcrowding and deplorable conditions. The County had to buy space from other counties. They brought in an expert that said that they needed to build another thousand beds right away. But we started training law enforcement officers in alternatives to jail and emergency rooms. We have a central health care, CMS, and we are bringing primary care. We grew by about three hundred and fifty thousand people last census. But now we have about a thousand empty beds in the county jail. I checked three weeks ago and we had 576 empty beds. Both our sheriff, a retired two star general, and our police chief require all their officers to go through the forty-hour crisis intervention training. We have twenty-five thousand people a year who are mainly brought to our Restoration Center rather than a jail or emergency room.

Colleen Horton
Policy Program Officer, Hogg Foundation for Mental Health

> *Colleen Horton is the Policy Program Officer at the Hogg Foundation for Mental Health at The University of Texas at Austin. Prior to moving to the foundation 5 years ago, Colleen spent 10 years as the director of public policy at the Texas Center for Disability Studies at the University of Texas. She has a graduate degree in public policy from the Lyndon B. Johnson School of Public Affairs. She served on the Texas Children's Policy Council for ten years and is currently a member of the*

state Medicaid Managed Care Advisory Committee, the Texas Medical Care Advisory Committee and the Promoting Independence Advisory Committee (Texas Olmstead advisory committee). Colleen is also on the national advisory board for the National Child Traumatic Stress Network and a member of the Institute of Medicine Forum on Promoting Children's Cognitive, Affective, and Behavioral Health. Colleen works extensively with state agencies, legislators, legislative staff and other advocates on issues affecting the mental health and wellness of adults and children.

I'm with the Hogg Foundation for mental health. The Foundation is part of the division of diversity and community engagement at the University of Texas. It was started in 1940 by the children of former Governor Hogg. We celebrated our seventy-fifth anniversary this year. Our primary goal for all seventy-five years, even if our name has changed, was to advance the mental wellness of Texans.

I want to make you all aware of a document that you might find helpful during this session. It's our guide to mental health systems and services in Texas. This is our second edition. We prepared one before the 83rd session as well, and it's our way of trying to provide information so that policy makers, staff, and advocates have some resource guide when they are making mental health decisions. We will be delivering one of these to each legislative office next week, and it is also available online.

We were asked whether we were throwing the right lifelines to people with mental illness. Lifelines typically imply that we are in a crisis, a situation where we need someone to save our lives. With mental health we need to look at a longer, wider continuum of services. We need to look at early intervention. We need to look at supporting people who are on the road to recovery, who are really working on their recovery plan and trying to become more reengaged with their community. But the question is here, so I'll answer it. Are we throwing the right lifelines? Yes, no, and sometimes we don't know. I'll try to give you an example of each of these situations.

However, especially during the Sunset process, we need to look at more than the big infrastructure changes. If you just take the same systems and put them in different boxes, it isn't reform and it is not going to improve anything. We need to dig down as we go through the Sunset process and get to the ground level. We need to really look at how the new system or structure will impact how we deliver services on the ground, in communities and in your districts. An example of something that we are doing right was the infusion of additional dollars. That helped in many ways. We do not have the data to tell us the outcomes, but we know what we needed. We know that people with serious mental illness, if they do not have housing, if they do not have a place to sleep at night or shower, then they will not be working on their recovery, or be able to manage their medications. The money that was appropriated to housing served over a thousand people and provided housing services for more than a thousand people with serious mental illness. We know that that is a good thing.

Then we have things like the YES waiver. The Youth Empowerment Services is a good thing that we are doing. However, it is the only Medicaid waiver that we have for mental health, and it only serves children. It is not statewide yet. There was a rider last session that directed the state to work on a plan to expand it statewide, but this waiver provides intensive community services to help prevent families from having to relinquish their child to Child Protective Services or the juvenile justice system, because they cannot get the comprehensive and intensive mental health services that they need. These are children of families who are really in crisis and need that level of help. We need to make sure that we keep moving forward with the expansion of the YES waiver. I believe that it is available in ten counties. Those ten counties represent about sixty percent of the population, but that leaves about 244 counties without the program. We need to make sure that we continue that. This was an example of some things that are not working well, and could be done better. We need to look at these and do them differently through the Sunset process.

One of these things is the way that we address the mental health needs of people with intellectual and developmental disabilities. For as long as I can remember we haven't talked about the mental health and wellness of people with intellectual disabilities. We talk about managing their behavior, making them compliant, what medications they need, but we don't look at what they are suffering from. These people experience trauma and mental illness at twice the rate of the general public. As we go forward and merge some agencies – right now we have disability over here and mental over there and never the two shall meet – we need to think of that level of service provision as we try and create this new infrastructure.

Another example of something that we need to improve is the practice of forcing parents to relinquish their child to the state if they need to get mental health services for that child. In my mind, that is one of the worst things that our state does. We have been working on it for a long time. We have made some progress, but not a lot. It is a very inequitable system. If I have a child with a developmental disability or intellectual disability then I am entitled to place that child in a nursing home or intermediate care facility or a state supported living center. The state pats me on the back and sends me home to get some rest. I do not lose my parental right and I get to continue making decisions about my child. If I'm that same parent and my child has a serious emotional disturbance or is a danger to himself or others, and I don't have the resources, I do not have the same rights. Oftentimes the only option is to relinquish that child to the state. They lose their rights as a parent. They have no more decision making power for their child, and on top of that, their names go on the central abuse and neglect registry. Even if there were no neglect and they simply needed the services. That is simply wrong. We need to fix that. It even makes fiscal sense. Once the child is relinquished, the state is paying for the mental health services, but it is also paying for conservatorship, sometimes for very long time periods.

We have over five hundred mental health specialists and over three hundred and fifty certified recovery coaches. These folks have done an incredible job. They are employed at all thirty-nine local mental health authorities and a number of state hospitals. The problem is that under our current system they can only be reimbursed for their services provided by a peer support specialist when they are providing rehabilitation services at a local mental health authority. That means that hospital ERs, integrated health care settings, community clinics, and criminal and juvenile justice settings cannot be reimbursed for those services. We really need to look where we direct the commission to identify what peer support services are, who can provide them, what the requirements are for certification, and for supervision. That is an economical and effective way to increase the support that the mental health work force receives.

Consumer directed services, or self-direction is another area that we have fallen behind in the mental health field. Many of you may have seen Kate's editorial where she talked about self-direction. We have had this type of direction for disabilities for over a decade, it is in all of their programs, their managed care. It makes even more sense on the mental health side, but it has lagged, with only one little pilot in the North Star area. We need to move forward on that.

Finally, I mentioned that it is hard to tell where we are, which is primarily because of the lack of data. It may be that we are too soon in the program to have quality comprehensive data or to be able to evaluate it. Perhaps we are not collecting the right data. The Department of State Health Services releases figures every quarter, they call it the data book. It has got gobs of numbers and figures and dollars. But we have not been measuring recovery outcomes. Are people getting better? Are they getting jobs? Do they have housing? Are they engaging in their community? Are they taking responsibility and managing their own recovery? We have ways to measure those things, and they will tell us if we are investing our money properly or not. We need to take a look and the Sunset process offers a great opportunity to do that.

The Hogg Foundation cannot lobby in the legislature, since we are part of the University of Texas, but we have spent thousands of hours working with legislators and staff, providing information, helping analyze bills, that sort of thing. Please call on us; we are here to help.

Andrew Keller
Executive Vice President for Policy and Programs,
Meadows Mental Health Policy Institute

> ANDREW KELLER, PHD, *is a licensed psychologist with more than 20 years of experience in behavioral health policy and particular expertise in health and human services integration, behavioral health financing, managed care systems and purchasing, and implementation of empirically supported practices for adults and children. Andy is a founding partner and senior consultant with TriWest Group, a health systems consulting firm. His work has centered on helping local systems implement evidence-based and innovative care, as well as helping local and state governments develop the regulatory and financial framework to support them. Prior to forming TriWest Group, Andy worked in Colorado at the health plan level with a leading Medicaid HMO and at the provider level with the Mental Health Center of Denver, helping develop care management systems for Denver's transition to a Medicaid managed care mental health system. Previously, he directed a range of community-based programs, including assertive community treatment, adult and child outpatient clinics, school-based and early childhood programs, and specialty programs for older adults and Latino communities. Andy is responsible for all behavioral health policy work and all policy deliverables of the Meadows Institute.*

I want to thank Kate and the folks at TPPF for putting this on the agenda. I think that it is actually very exciting that you all are doing this. Especially considering that you only have a very limited amount of time to focus on issues in these three days. It is important to get folks aware of these issues. I think that we have got people's attention recognizing a lot of the needs that Leon talked about. This topic is really pertinent.

The comic that you spoke of Kate is really pertinent as well. We all have good ideas, and no one here gets into this business because we want to hurt people. We want to help and make things better. Often, however, the unintended consequences of those actions that get people, and that is what I am going to talk about today, as well as to give a framework that we have developed at the Mental Health Policy Institute. Like Colleen, we do not lobby, but we respond to requests for information. I also liked, Colleen, how you talked about lifelines and the tendency to fixate on crises.

Seymour Sarason was one of the first folks in community mental health who talked about prevention and used a metaphor. We are constantly pulling people out of the river just before they go over a waterfall, but we never try to keep from people going into the river. That is a very pertinent metaphor. We spend a lot of energy building best practice crisis services over the last decade. However, increasingly, we have a system that rotates people through crisis, rotates, people through jail, but does not keep them in care very well. I am going to talk about a framework where we can try to move forward. Colleen and Leon's points about outcomes being critical are right on. There is a lot of data out there. We know that fifty percent of mental illnesses manifest themselves by the age of fourteen. That means hat it manifests in childhood. Most of the last fifty percent manifest by the time that we are twenty-one. That is a huge developmental time during which bipolar disorders, schizophrenia, and other disorders kick in. We are talking about very young people.

We have some data that we are going to be releasing later this month, our own public polling data, where we see that actually eight in ten Texans have a close family member or person close to them that is currently being affected by mental health and substance abuse. That is the same rate of people that have a family member or close friend with cancer. Think about the difference between those scenarios. If I had a child with cancer, I'd probably tell my church, my support group. If they knew that my child was going in for treatment, they would make me casseroles and they would be offering support. However, if my kid was depressed, I would not tell them. I wouldn't want them to single my child out for that. I would not want them bringing me casseroles. They would be awkwardly silent. It is important that we find out how to move beyond that. How do we move into a realm where we can help?

I am going to give you a five-point framework that we are going to use to think about this. First, Texans deserve care that works. We need to know what the right lifelines are, because they deserve care that works. That means that care has to be efficient, effective, and the right care. One of my colleagues is a psychologist and firefighter, and he points out that CPR is an evidence-based practice. However, when he is responding to an emergency, and ran in and did CPR on everyone there, then he would break a lot of ribs, hurt a lot of people, and have a lot of people die unnecessarily. Not everyone needs CPR. In Texas, we are famous for restricting our providers. We tell them the three evidence-based practices and let them know that they can do these and we'll remunerate them, but only if they do two hours of them. If they perform less, then we know that they are not efficient because everyone in Texas needs CPR for two hours. This is ridiculous.

There are hundreds of "right lifelines." How do we move beyond the idea that you can only have one or two? How do we build an accountability system where we are measuring the effects of treatment? One thing that we have to do is make sure that state purchasing is accountable to Texas taxpayers. Notice that I said Texas taxpayers. When you are thinking about how to spend the state taxpayer's money, you need to think about local taxpayers who have to run jails and emergency rooms. There is not one person that you can ask in state governments about how much we spend on mental health. They do not know how many people spend it, because it is not any one person's job. Some people think that Dr. Laki (PH) is responsible; others think that it is Lauren Lacefield Lewis, who runs the mental health and substance abuse division. However, she only controls about 1.3 billion dollars when there is a billion more dollars being spent that she has no responsibility for and therefore has very little knowledge about.

That is one benefit of the Sunset review; providing a point of accountability. There is one behavioral health division and there should be legislation that ensures that we have one person who knows how much is spent in the state. How could we have accountability if we do not know how much we spend? Then we need to know how many people we are serving. We know how many people we serve through DSHS, but most people do not know that we serve about a hundred and eighty thousand people with big three diagnoses through Medicaid. There is only about a seventy or eighty thousand people in overlap. We don't know how many people we have not accounted for, but we are doing some research that will be released later this month through Dr. Rowan's group at UT Houston that will give us a better idea. Keep in mind that there is about two billion dollars being spent on emergency department care and jails at the local level.

This needs to be coordinated, and it needs more than one bill, it needs a legislative oversight committee. The third principle that we want people to keep in mind is that health care is local. No one delivers health care at the capital. Health care happens through local providers like Leon. There is a report that came out estimating that we need five hundred more beds at state hospitals. Should we just start building beds, or talk with the local mental health authorities and ask, "Do you want to spend the money on hospital beds or on sidewalks or bridges or peer support?" There are a lot of things that keep people out of hospitals. There are a million people with serious mental illness in Texas, it would cost two hundred billion dollars a year to put everybody with mental illness in a hospital. I know that no one wants to do that.

Before we do that we need to have a community conversation and involve the local level. The fourth principle is an emphasis on purchasing meaningful outcomes. Let me give you an example of how not to do that. Leon runs one of the best homeless services in the country. The metric was a big accomplishment of the last legislative session. But we decided we would use it to measure homelessness the same way in every part of Texas. There are not equal numbers of homeless people in Hudspeth County as there are here in Austin. Not only that, we look at one single funding stream, who is paid for by DSHS. We say that you need to reduce the number of people that are on that funding stream below a certain level. The easiest way to achieve that outcome is to quit serving homeless people. Leon did not do that and he was penalized several hundred thousand dollars. He was penalized in the exact same year that we rolled out a ten million dollar statewide program that was modeled on his program.

These are four of the principles. The fifth I will say briefly because I am out of time. The fifth is addressing our work force emergency. We cannot improve on any of these principles unless we have a work force. We need to do an emergency investment in our work force, both with long-term solutions as well as short-term efforts, like some of our owners' lack of reciprocity. There are a lot of things that we can do and I think that these five principles will get us closer to having the right lifelines.

Q&A

QUESTION: You mentioned using some of the recovery patients to attract homeless people into wherever you take care of them. The first thing I thought of was Alcoholics Anonymous. The main leaders of that understand alcoholics. Can you take that model and use it?

LEON EVANS: You can and we do. Let me tell you about it. Remember that we asked Mr. Greehey to go work with the representative and the senate and get some money? We added a sobering and detox unit.

In San Antonio, there were a lot of homeless people downtown that were aggressively panhandling, getting arrested for passing out on the street, urinating or defecating in public, these petty crimes. They would get arrested and would go through the magistration process. The city of San Antonio spent about sixteen million dollars in magistration. That was a big percent of the cost of this group. They threw them in the drunk take after giving them fines which they would never pay. Law enforcement would let you sober up so that the people do not go into convulsions and dying or they will have to pay – in fact have already paid – several million dollar lawsuits. Then they released them. These people leave and start self-medicating again. They go back to panhandling and drinking and drugs. They may be arrested three or four times. They have no insurance and they are impaired. They would never get any help. Their illness has been so painful for family and friends that they do not have anyone to advocate for them.

Now we have all of these cops that are trained in mental health and we have developed a sobering unit. This means that they bring them to use, they do not take them to jail or magistration unless they have committed a major crime. Everyone in that unit is on recovery. It is a medically supervised unit, but it is not a medical model, so the cost is very low. We used to have beds but people fell and hurt themselves, and now we have mattresses on the floor. Our staff bath people, they treat them with dignity and respect. They let them know, "Hey, I used to be sick like you. Do you want to go to detox?" About twenty percent say yes. Detox is a necessary intervention which we know doesn't work too well. The important issue is maintaining your sobriety after your detox. On that homeless campus it is alcohol and drug free, and we have two dorms that operate. They are an in-house, ninety-day recovery program. You would be in there long enough to learn what your disease has done to you, your family, and your children. It is also long enough for your brain chemistry to kick back in. We use best practices in alcohol and drug treatment. Then we hook people up with AA and NA. About sixty to seventy percent of the people in these programs are still clean and sober a year later. Most are working, living independently.

There are models to use if we had the flexibility. When we first did the unit, districts had no standard for sobering. They made us license all of the beds as detox. Their rules said that we had to have a waiting list. That would not work, so we defied the state. I took a bunch of detox beds offline and made them sobering. Now the state takes credit for this because it is a model program and works well. I have talked about a few things such as childrens' services. We developed the first curriculum in the US for school police. School police are usually right out of the academy, trying to earn their command presence and they are an entry level position because they do not pay as well. You may have a young officer with a teacher who is asking them to come get a kid that they never want to see again and the officer is charging forward and gets in a kid's face that is emotionally disturbed or mentally ill and then there is an altercation. Then the kid goes to juvenile detention or is kicked out of school. He becomes estranged from the community and becomes a truant, perhaps becomes involved with a gang.

But now these cops are trained to recognize that this kid has an emotional disturbance. They use de-escalation techniques. They call the family and get the kid help. One of our 1115 district projects is a children's crisis unit. It just now opened and is already working well.

This last session we took all of the rehab services away from the community of behavioral health, the mental health authorities, and it was turned over to the NCOs. I want to take about disconnect in state government. You have DSHS over here that decides that we will do a new assessment. It is the Adult Needs and Strengths Assessment (ANSA). When we do this adult assessment we talk about the positive things about people that have severe mental illness. We do not talk about their multiple admissions to state hospitals and how dysfunctional they are and how they do not have supports. Then the NCO doctors look at our assessments and say, "There is nothing wrong with this person, I am not going to authorize that service." This strength-based assessment is not giving the right picture to the funder.

KATE MURPHY: Mental health is going to be such an important policy issue this legislative session. We are so glad we could be part of the discussion on it. If you have questions, I'm sure our panelists would be happy to stay and answer. Please feel free to contact me at TPPF if you have any questions regarding mental health and our stances on it. I'd like to thank our panelists, Leon Evans, Colleen Horton, and Dr. Andy Keller, for taking the time to come and share their experience, their expertise, we really appreciate it and I hope you all enjoy the rest of policy orientation.

About Right on Crime

Right on Crime is a national campaign to promote successful, conservative solutions on American criminal justice policy—reforming the system to ensure public safety, shrink government, and save taxpayers money. By sharing research and policy ideas and mobilizing strong conservative voices, we work to raise awareness of the growing support for effective reforms within the conservative movement. We are transforming the debate on criminal justice in America.

Our Statement Of Principles

As members of the nation's conservative movement, we strongly support constitutionally limited government, transparency, individual liberty, personal responsibility, and free enterprise. We believe public safety is a core responsibility of government because the establishment of a well-functioning criminal justice system enforces order and respect for every person's right to property and life, and ensures that liberty does not lead to license.

Conservatives correctly insist that government services be evaluated on whether they produce the best possible results at the lowest possible cost, but too often this lens of accountability has not focused as much on public safety policies as other areas of government. As such, corrections spending has expanded to become the second fastest growing area of state budgets—trailing only Medicaid.

Conservatives are known for being tough on crime, but we must also be tough on criminal justice spending. That means demanding more cost-effective approaches that enhance public safety. A clear example is our reliance on prisons, which serve a critical role by incapacitating dangerous offenders and career criminals but are not the solution for every type of offender. And in some instances, they have the unintended consequence of hardening nonviolent, low-risk offenders—making them a greater risk to the public than when they entered.

Applying the following conservative principles to criminal justice policy is vital to achieving a cost-effective system that protects citizens, restores victims, and reforms wrongdoers.

1. As with any government program, the criminal justice system must be transparent and include performance measures that hold it account- able for its results in protecting the public, lowering crime rates, reducing re-offending, collecting victim restitution and conserving taxpayers' money.

2. Crime victims, along with the public and taxpayers, are among the key "consumers" of the criminal justice system; the victim's conception of justice, public safety, and the offender's risk for future criminal conduct should be prioritized when determining an appropriate punishment.

3. The corrections system should emphasize public safety, personal responsibility, work, restitution, community service, and treatment— both in probation and parole, which supervise most offenders, and in prisons.

4. An ideal criminal justice system works to reform amenable offenders who will return to society through harnessing the power of families, charities, faith-based groups, and communities.

5. Because incentives affect human behavior, policies for both offenders and the corrections system must align incentives with our goals of public safety, victim restitution and satisfaction, and cost-effectiveness, thereby moving from a system that grows when it fails to one that rewards results.

6. Criminal law should be reserved for conduct that is either blameworthy or threatens public safety, not wielded to grow government and undermine economic freedom.

These principles are grounded in time-tested conservative truths—constitutionally limited government, transparency, individual liberty, personal responsibility, free enterprise, and the centrality of the family and community. All of these are critical to addressing today's criminal justice challenges. It is time to apply these principles to the task of delivering a better return on taxpayers' investments in public safety. Our security, prosperity, and freedom depend on it.

Right on Crime Signatories

Newt Gingrich
Former Speaker of the House of Representatives

Grover Norquist
Americans for Tax Reform

Gov. Rick Perry
Former Governor of Texas

Gov. Asa Hutchinson
Governor of Arkansas

Chuck Colson (1931-2012)
Prison Fellowship Ministries

William J. Bennett
Former Secretary of Education and Federal "Drug Czar"

Jeb Bush
Former Governor of Florida

Ken Cuccinelli
Former Attorney General, Virginia

David Keene
Former Chairman, American Conservative Union and National Rifle Association

J.C. Watts
Former Member of the U.S. House of Representatives, Oklahoma's 4th District

Edwin Meese III
Former U.S. Attorney General

Stephen Moore
The Heritage Foundation

Pat Nolan
Director, Criminal Justice Reform Project, American Conservative Union Foundation

Richard Viguerie
ConservativeHQ.com

Brooke Rollins
Texas Public Policy Foundation

Ken Blackwell
Former Ohio Secretary of State

Ralph Reed
Founder, Faith and Freedom Coalition

Eli Lehrer
R Street Institute

Rebecca Hagelin
Executive Committee, Council for National Policy

Tony Perkins
Family Research Council

B. Wayne Hughes, Jr.
Businessman and Philanthropist

Henry Juszkiewicz
CEO of Gibson Guitar

Penny Nance
Concerned Women for America

John J. DiLulio, Jr.

University of Pennsylvania

Ward Connerly
American Civil Rights Institute

George Kelling
Manhattan Institute

Gary Bauer
American Values

David Barton
WallBuilders

Rabbi Daniel Lapin
American Alliance of Jews and Christians

Michael Reagan
The Reagan Legacy Foundation

Monica Crowley, Ph.D.
Fox News political analyst

Erick Erickson
Founder of RedState.com

Alfred Regnery
Law Enforcement Legal Defense Fund

Viet Dinh
Georgetown University Law Center, former U.S. Assistant Attorney General

Ronald F. Scheberle
American Legislative Exchange Council

Larry Thompson
Former U.S. Deputy Attorney General

Deborah Daniels
Former U.S. Attorney and Assistant U.S. Attorney General

Donald Devine
Former Director, Office of Personnel Management

Richard Doran
Former Florida Attorney General

Jim Petro
Former Ohio Attorney General

Hal Stratton
Former New Mexico Attorney General

Joe Whitley
Former Acting U.S. Associate Attorney General and U.S. Attorney

BJ Nikkel
Former Majority Whip, Colorado House of Representatives

Kris Steele
Former Speaker, Oklahoma House of Representatives

Allan Bense
Former Speaker, Florida House of Representatives

For a more complete list of Right on Crime signatories—including state-based signatories and partners—see rightoncrime.com

The Conservative Case for Criminal Justice Reform

PUBLIC SAFETY. Because government exists to secure liberties that can only be enjoyed to the extent there is public safety, state and local policymakers must make fighting crime their top priority, including utilizing prisons to incapacitate violent offenders and career criminals. Prisons are overused, however, when nonviolent offenders who may be safely supervised in the community are given lengthy sentences. Prisons provide diminishing returns when such offenders emerge more disposed to re-offend than when they entered prison.

RIGHT-SIZING GOVERNMENT. Nearly 1 in every 100 American adults is in prison or jail. When you add in those on probation or parole, almost 1 in 33 adults is under some type of control by the criminal justice system. When Ronald Reagan was president, the total correctional control rate was 1 in every 77 adults. This represents a significant expansion of government power. By reducing excessive sentence lengths and holding nonviolent offenders accountable through prison alternatives, public safety can often be achieved consistent with a legitimate, but more limited, role for government.

FISCAL DISCIPLINE. The prison system now costs states more than $50 billion per year, up from $11 billion in the mid-1980s. It has been the second-fastest growing area of state budgets, trailing only Medicaid, and consumes one in every 14 general fund dollars. Conservatives must address runaway spending on prisons just as they do with education and health care, subjecting the same level of skepticism and scrutiny to all expenditures of taxpayers' funds.

VICTIM SUPPORT. In 2008, Texas probationers paid $45 million in restitution to victims, but prisoners paid less than $500,000 in restitution, fines, and fees. Making victims whole must be prioritized when determining appropriate punishments for offenders. The criminal justice system should be structured to ensure that victims are treated with dignity and respect and that they may participate in the criminal justice process and receive restitution.

PERSONAL RESPONSIBILITY. With some 5 million offenders on probation or parole, it's critical that the corrections system hold these offenders accountable for their actions by holding a job or performing community service, attending required treatment programs, and staying crime- and drug-free. When the system has real teeth, the results can be dramatic: offenders subject to swift, certain and commensurate sanctions for rule violations in Hawaii's HOPE program are less than half as likely to be arrested or fail a drug test.

GOVERNMENT ACCOUNTABILITY. More than 40 percent of released offenders return to prison within three years of release, and in some states, recidivism rates are closer to 60 percent. As Right on Crime signatories Newt Gingrich and Mark Earley have asked, "[i]f two-thirds of public school students dropped out, or two-thirds of all bridges built collapsed within three years, would citizens tolerate it?" Corrections funding should be partly linked to outcomes and should implement proven strategies along the spectrum between basic probation and prison.

FAMILY PRESERVATION. According to National Review, "40 percent of low-income men who father a child out of wedlock have already been in jail or prison by the time their first son or daughter is born." The family unit is the foundation of society. In a society in which too many young men are incarcerated, marriage rates are depressed and far too many children grow up in single-parent homes. Instead of harming families, the corrections system must harness the power of charities, faith-based groups, and communities to reform offenders and preserve families.

FREE ENTERPRISE. The Constitution lists only three federal crimes, but the number of statutory federal crimes has now swelled to around 4,500. This is to say nothing of the thousands of bizarre state-level crimes, such as the 11 felonies in Texas related to the harvesting of oysters. The explosion of non-traditional criminal laws grows government and undermines economic freedom. Criminal law should be reserved for conduct that is blameworthy or threatens public safety, not wielded to regulate non-fraudulent economic activity involving legal products.

www.ingramcontent.com/pod-product-compliance
Lightning Source LLC
Chambersburg PA
CBHW021547200526
45163CB00016B/2886